Reading & Writing Companion

Living the Dream

What does home mean to you?

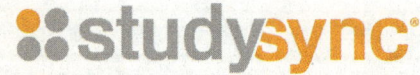

studysync.com

Copyright © BookheadEd Learning, LLC
All Rights Reserved.

Send all inquiries to:
BookheadEd Learning, LLC
610 Daniel Young Drive
Sonoma, CA 95476

No part of this publication may be reproduced or transmitted in any form, by any means, electronic or mechanical, including photocopy, recording, or utilized by any information storage or retrieval system, without written permission from BookheadEd Learning, LLC.

ISBN 978-1-94-973907-7

2 3 4 5 6 LMN 24 23 22 21 20
B

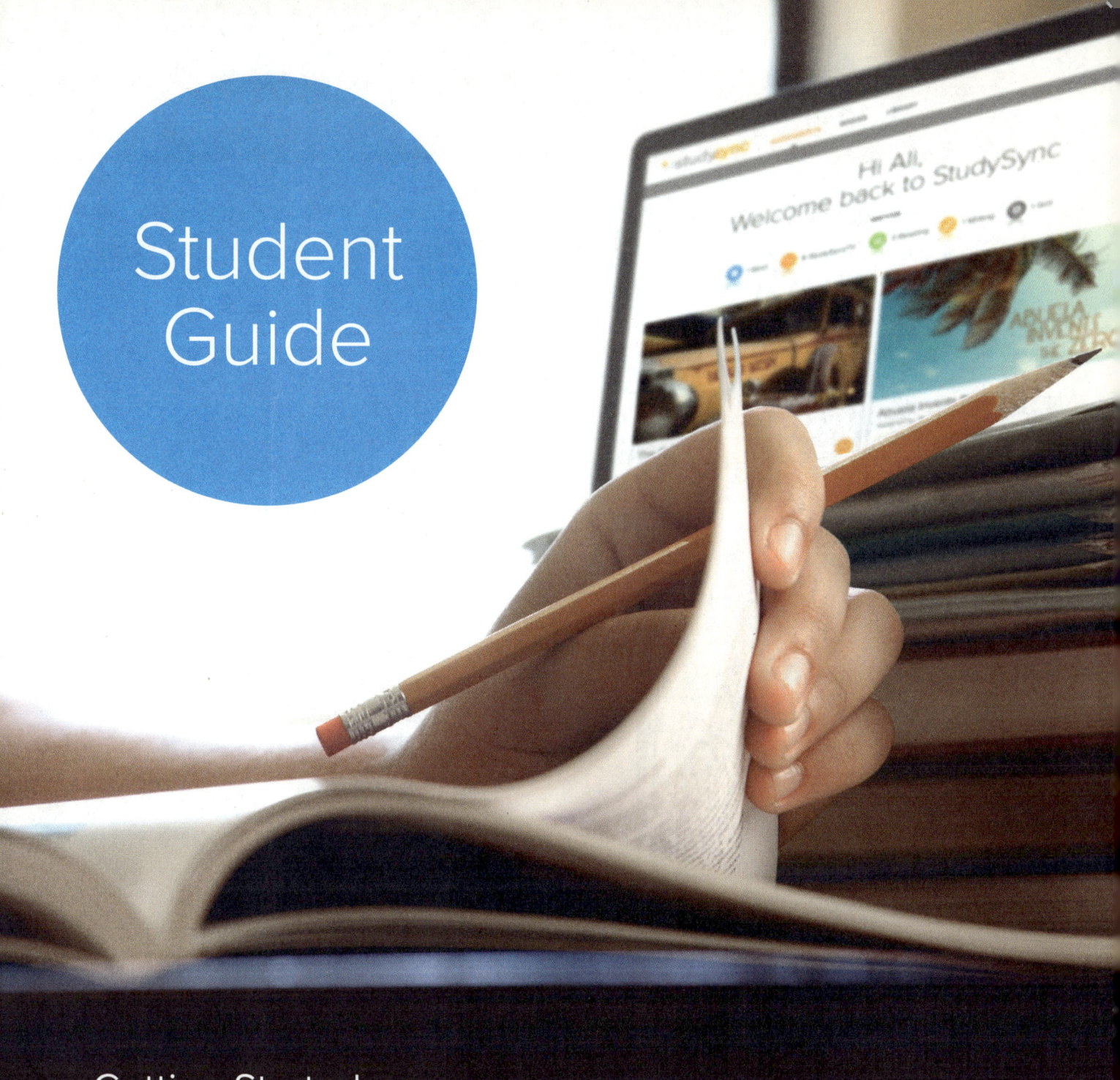

Student Guide

Getting Started

Welcome to the StudySync Reading & Writing Companion! In this book, you will find a collection of readings based on the theme of the unit you are studying. As you work through the readings, you will be asked to answer questions and perform a variety of tasks designed to help you closely analyze and understand each text selection. Read on for an explanation of each section of this book.

Close Reading and Writing Routine

In each unit, you will read texts that share a common theme, despite their different genres, time periods, and authors. Each reading encourages a closer look through questions and a short writing assignment.

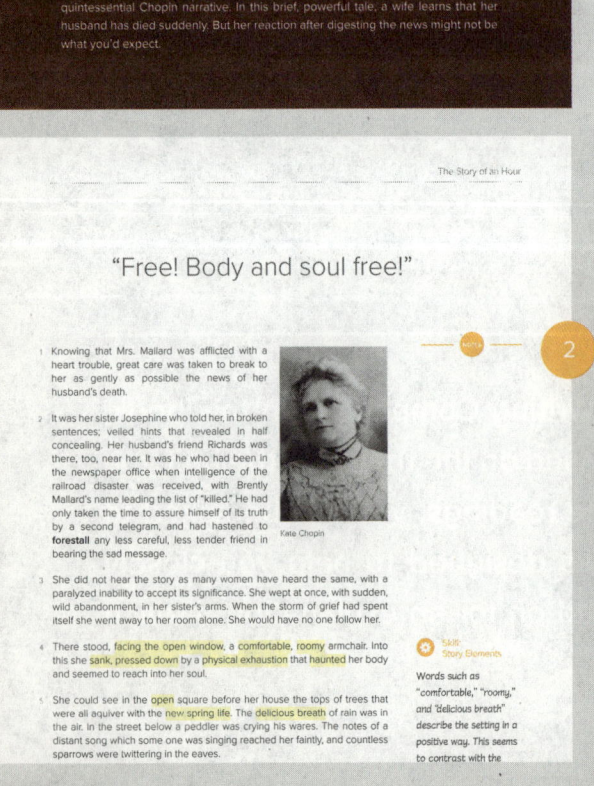

1. Introduction

An Introduction to each text provides historical context for your reading as well as information about the author. You will also learn about the genre of the text and the year in which it was written.

2. Notes

Many times, while working through the activities after each text, you will be asked to **annotate** or **make annotations** about what you are reading. This means that you should highlight or underline words in the text and use the "Notes" column to make comments or jot down any questions you have. You may also want to note any unfamiliar vocabulary words here.

You will also see sample student annotations to go along with the Skill lesson for that text.

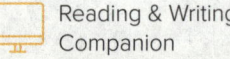

Reading & Writing Companion

③ First Read

During your first reading of each selection, you should just try to get a general idea of the content and message of the reading. Don't worry if there are parts you don't understand or words that are unfamiliar to you. You'll have an opportunity later to dive deeper into the text.

④ Think Questions

These questions will ask you to start thinking critically about the text, asking specific questions about its purpose, and making connections to your prior knowledge and reading experiences. To answer these questions, you should go back to the text and draw upon specific evidence to support your responses. You will also begin to explore some of the more challenging vocabulary words in the selection.

⑤ Skills

Each Skill includes two parts: Checklist and Your Turn. In the Checklist, you will learn the process for analyzing the text. The model student annotations in the text provide examples of how you might make your own notes following the instructions in the Checklist. In the Your Turn, you will use those same instructions to practice the skill.

Reading & Writing Companion   v

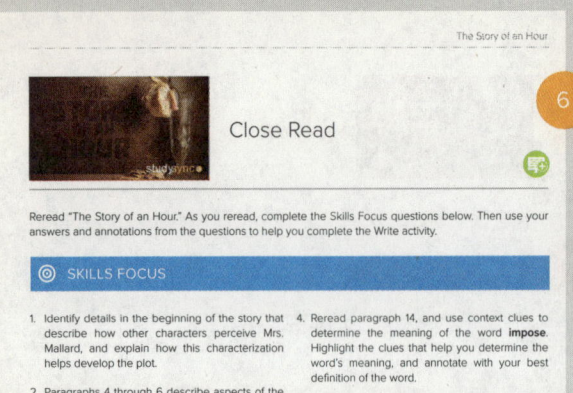

Close Read & Skills Focus

After you have completed the First Read, you will be asked to go back and read the text more closely and critically. Before you begin your Close Read, you should read through the Skills Focus to get an idea of the concepts you will want to focus on during your second reading. You should work through the Skills Focus by making annotations, highlighting important concepts, and writing notes or questions in the "Notes" column. Depending on instructions from your teacher, you may need to respond online or use a separate piece of paper to start expanding on your thoughts and ideas.

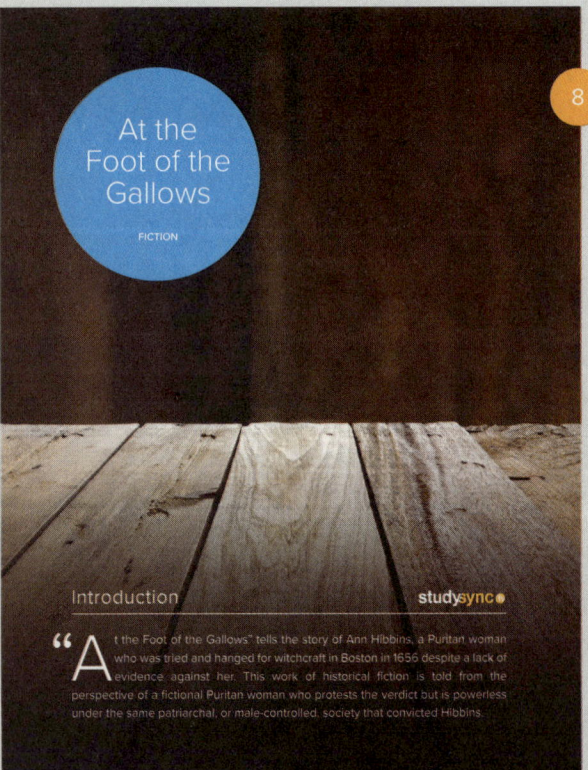

Write

Your study of each selection will end with a writing assignment. For this assignment, you should use your notes, annotations, personal ideas, and answers to both the Think and Skills Focus questions. Be sure to read the prompt carefully and address each part of it in your writing.

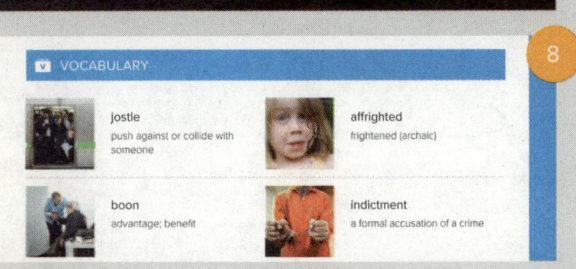

English Language Learner

The English Language Learner texts focus on improving language proficiency. You will practice learning strategies and skills in individual and group activities to become better readers, writers, and speakers.

Extended Writing Project and Grammar

This is your opportunity to use genre characteristics and craft to compose meaningful, longer written works exploring the theme of each unit. You will draw information from your readings, research, and own life experiences to complete the assignment.

1 Writing Project

After you have read all of the unit text selections, you will move on to a writing project. Each project will guide you through the process of writing your essay. Student models will provide guidance and help you organize your thoughts. One unit ends with an **Extended Oral Project** which will give you an opportunity to develop your oral language and communication skills.

2 Writing Process Steps

There are four steps in the writing process: Plan, Draft, Revise, and Edit and Publish. During each step, you will form and shape your writing project, and each lesson's peer review will give you the chance to receive feedback from your peers and teacher.

3 Writing Skills

Each Skill lesson focuses on a specific strategy or technique that you will use during your writing project. Each lesson presents a process for applying the skill to your own work and gives you the opportunity to practice it to improve your writing.

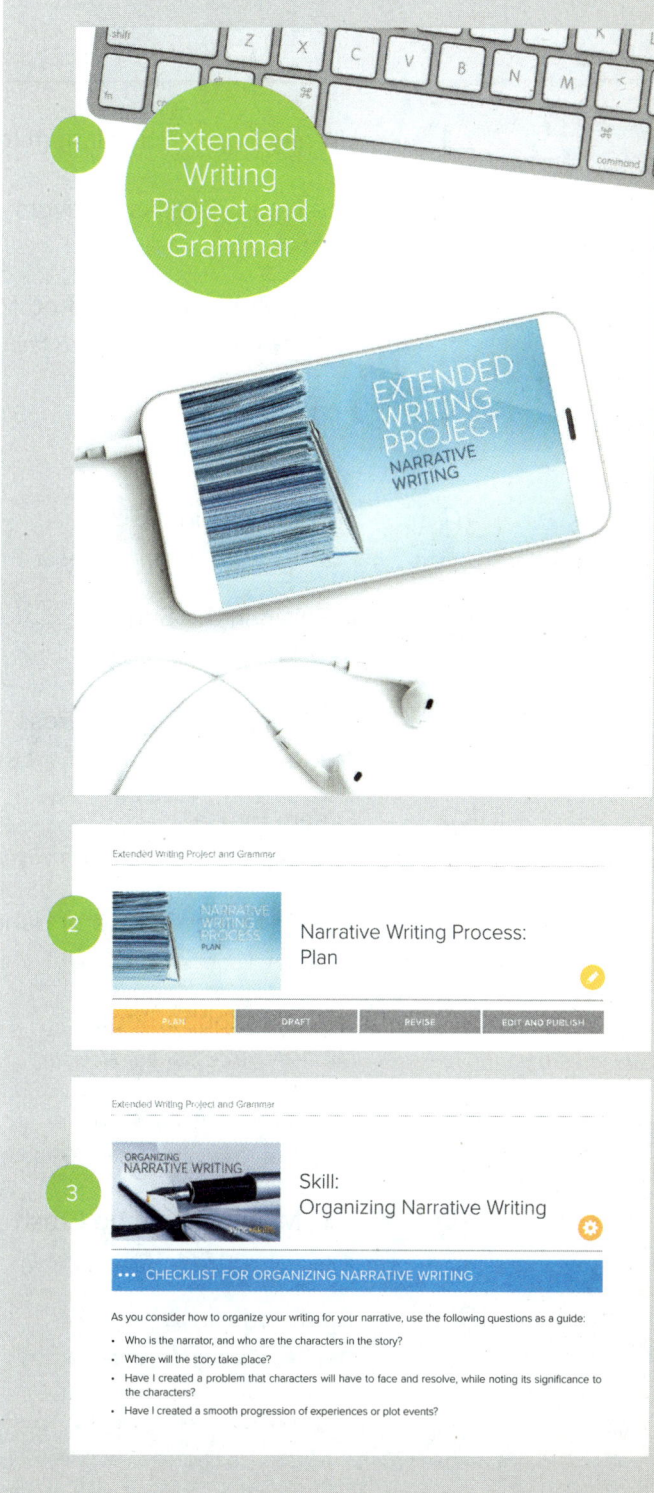

Living the Dream

What does home mean to you?

Genre Focus: **DRAMA**

Texts

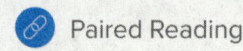 Paired Readings

1   Literary Focus: The Harlem Renaissance

8   The Negro Speaks of Rivers
POETRY *Langston Hughes*

11   How It Feels to Be Colored Me
INFORMATIONAL TEXT *Zora Neale Hurston*

24   Fences
DRAMA *August Wilson*

36   The Old Cabin
POETRY *Paul Laurence Dunbar*

40   A Raisin in the Sun
DRAMA *Lorraine Hansberry*

50   Letter from Chief John Ross
ARGUMENTATIVE TEXT *John Ross*

62   Dream House
ARGUMENTATIVE TEXT *StudySync*

69   The Fall of the House of Usher
FICTION *Edgar Allan Poe*

86   In Our Neighborhood
FICTION *Alice Dunbar-Nelson*

94   The Yellow Wallpaper
FICTION *Charlotte Perkins Gilmore*

119   Eat, Memory: Orange Crush
INFORMATIONAL TEXT *Yiyun Li*

123   Boyhood
DRAMA *Richard Linklater*

Reading & Writing Companion

Please note that excerpts and passages in the StudySync® library and this workbook are intended as touchstones to generate interest in an author's work. The excerpts and passages do not substitute for the reading of entire texts, and StudySync® strongly recommends that students seek out and purchase the whole literary or informational work in order to experience it as the author intended. Links to online resellers are available in our digital library. In addition, complete works may be ordered through an authorized reseller by filling out and returning to StudySync® the order form enclosed in this workbook.

Extended Writing Project and Grammar

133 | Plan
Planning Research
Evaluating Sources
Research and Notetaking

151 | Draft
Critiquing Research
Paraphrasing
Sources and Citations
Print and Graphic Features

166 | Revise
Using a Style Guide
Grammar: Contested usage
Grammar: Hyphens

174 | Edit and Publish

English Language Learner Resources

176 | Fighting for Justice
INFORMATIONAL TEXT

186 | Home Is Where the Heart Is
DRAMA

198 | Text Fulfillment through StudySync

Please note that excerpts and passages in the StudySync® library and this workbook are intended as touchstones to generate interest in an author's work. The excerpts and passages do not substitute for the reading of entire texts, and StudySync® strongly recommends that students seek out and purchase the whole literary or informational work in order to experience it as the author intended. Links to online resellers are available in our digital library. In addition, complete works may be ordered through an authorized reseller by filling out and returning to StudySync® the order form enclosed in this workbook.

Reading & Writing Companion

Unit 4: Living the Dream
What does home mean to you?

PAUL LAURENCE DUNBAR

Born the son of formerly enslaved parents from Kentucky, Paul Laurence Dunbar (1872–1906) published his first poem before he graduated from high school. Dunbar briefly worked as an editor for the *Dayton Tattler*, a newspaper published by classmate Orville Wright. Unable to afford law school, and rejected by newspapers because of the color of his skin, Dunbar became an elevator operator. He wrote in his spare time, self-published the collection *Oak and Ivy*, published poems and essays in newspapers nationwide, and eventually achieved international acclaim.

ALICE DUNBAR-NELSON

Activist and author Alice Dunbar-Nelson (1875–1935) was born in New Orleans, Louisiana, and began her schoolteacher career after graduating Straight University in 1892. Three years later, she published her first collection of short stories and poems, *Violets and Other Tales*. She later became politically active and helped organize for the women's suffrage movement. In 1918 she worked for the Woman's Committee of the Council of Defense, and in 1924 she campaigned for the Dyer Anti-Lynching Bill. She died in Philadelphia at the age of sixty.

CHARLOTTE PERKINS GILMAN

After having her first child, Charlotte Perkins Gilman (1860–1935) documented her depression in her diary. Her doctor prescribed the Rest Cure, which included having her child with her all the time, limiting "intellectual life" to two hours a day, and never writing again. Gilman's anxiety and depression and the prescribed cure inspired her short story "The Yellow Wallpaper." Her depression lifted when she divorced her husband and moved to California. She became involved in the feminist and women's suffrage movements, and lectured across the country.

LORRAINE HANSBERRY

Lorraine Hansberry (1930–1965) was born in the South Side of Chicago to a prominent African American family that called W. E. B. Du Bois, Langston Hughes, and Duke Ellington friends. Her father had founded one of Chicago's first banks for African Americans, yet the family faced opposition when they bought a new home. They had to move in secret and face a white mob that threw bricks through their window in a case that went to the Supreme Court. This experience laid the groundwork for Hansberry's Tony Award-winning play *A Raisin in the Sun*.

LANGSTON HUGHES

When his parents divorced and his father fled to Mexico, Langston Hughes (1902–1967) lived with his grandmother in Lawrence, Kansas, while his mother traveled seeking work. Of that time, he noted in his 1940 autobiography *The Big Sea*, "I began to believe in nothing but books and the wonderful world in books - where if people suffered, they suffered in beautiful language, not in monosyllables, as we did in Kansas." Hughes went on to attend Columbia University and sailed around West Africa before becoming a leader of the Harlem Renaissance.

ZORA NEALE HURSTON

When Zora Neale Hurston (1891–1960) was growing up in the all-black town of Eatonville, Florida, she only encountered white people when they passed through the town on their way to or from Orlando. Hurston studied anthropology at Howard, Barnard, and Columbia before dedicating herself to literature, experiences that later informed her writing on race and identity. Referencing her time at Barnard, she wrote, "I feel most colored when I am thrown against a sharp white background."

YIYUN LI

Beijing-born author Yiyun Li (b. 1972) has been published in *The New Yorker* and *The Paris Review*. After completing college, she moved to the United States in 1996. In 2000, Li began studies at the Iowa Writers' Workshop, where she earned her MFA. Her first short story collection, *A Thousand Years of Good Prayers*, received many awards, including the PEN/Hemingway Award. In 2007, Granta named her one of the best young American novelists, and in 2010 she was named to the New Yorker's "20 under 40" list for fiction. Li lives in Oakland, California.

RICHARD LINKLATER

Born in Texas, Richard Linklater (b. 1960) is an American filmmaker and story-teller. A college dropout, Linklater wrote, directed and produced *Dazed and Confused* (1993), a film that captured the angst of teenagers on their last day of high school. In 2002, he began filming *Boyhood*, a magnum opus that took over a decade to make. The film, released in 2014, tracks the coming of age of one boy and his absent father, with a cast that ages through the film. *Boyhood* won the Golden Globe for Best Motion Picture, Drama, and Linklater won Best Director.

EDGAR ALLAN POE

Edgar Allan Poe (1809–1949) may be best known for his poetry and his short stories, including "The Fall of the House of Usher," but he also wrote a novel. *The Narrative of Arthur Gordon Pym of Nantucket* (1838) tells the story of a young man, Pym, intoxicated by the prospect of the open sea. Pym becomes a stowaway on a whaling ship that suffers a mutiny by its crew and weathers a violent storm. Written as a "found text," the novel was later referred to by one scholar as "one of the most elusive major texts of American literature." Poe died at the age of forty.

CHIEF JOHN ROSS

Chief John Ross (1790–1866), born to a Cherokee mother and a Scottish father, served in a Cherokee regiment during the War of 1812 and is best known for his role negotiating on behalf of his people against the US government, which sought their relocation. In 1828, he was permanently elected principal chief of the Cherokee. Chief Ross's wife was among the nearly 25% of the Cherokee people who perished during the government's infamous Trail of Tears forced march. Chief Ross died in Washington, DC, on a trip to negotiate terms after the Civil War.

AUGUST WILSON

August Wilson (1945–2005) was born in Pittsburg, Pennsylvania, the fourth of seven children. At sixteen years old, he dropped out of school to work, but visited the library when he could. Between reading the pages of books, especially the works of Langston Hughes, Wilson discovered his passion and decided to become a writer, much to his mother's dismay. Wilson eventually helped establish a theater company, moved to Minnesota, worked as a chef to finance his art, and went on to win two Pulitzer Prizes for his plays *Fences* and *The Piano Lesson*.

LITERARY FOCUS:
The Harlem Renaissance

Introduction

This informational text offers background information about the historical and cultural circumstances that led to the Harlem Renaissance. After the turn of the 20th century, populations were becoming increasingly urban. African Americans living in Northern cities faced widespread discriminatory practices by city landlords, and those living in the South dealt with the racism and injustice of Jim Crow laws. This oppression, along with the North's newfound need for factory workers, led to both the Great Migration and a migration within New York City to the welcoming Harlem area. Partially a response to racist stereotyping and partially to the horror of the first World War, the Harlem Renaissance was an African American-led artistic movement that came to define the 1920s and early '30s and inspired generations of creative minds to come.

Literary Focus: The Harlem Renaissance

"How do artists of the Harlem Renaissance continue to inspire music and culture today?"

1   The Harlem Renaissance was a cultural movement among African Americans in New York City in the 1920s and 1930s. Musicians, writers, and other African American artists were drawn to the Harlem section of Manhattan by plentiful housing. The artistic outpouring lasted until the Great Depression, which forced many Harlem artists to move elsewhere to look for work. The impact of the Harlem Renaissance, however, can still be felt heavily in our culture today.

The Emergence of an African American Community

2   African Americans in New York City began moving to the Harlem area in about 1900. They were eager to move out of the West Side of Manhattan because of the overcrowded apartment buildings and increasing hostility from white neighbors. Harlem had a surplus of apartments, so landlords were eager to welcome African American tenants. When African-American churches began to relocate to Harlem as well, the population of African Americans became solidly established and continued to grow.

3   **Segregation** was widespread in the North as well as the South in the early 1900s. African Americans were banned from many white-owned businesses, including restaurants and hotels. As a result, African Americans started their own businesses to draw on the large number of potential customers in their neighborhood. Among the most successful businesses were nightclubs that featured jazz and blues.

The Great Migration

4   *The Great Migration* is a term that refers to the movement of African Americans from the South to large cities in the North between approximately 1916 and 1940 in its first wave. World War I cut off the flow of European immigrants to the United States. Northern factories were growing and needed more workers. They recruited African Americans from the South to help make up for the shortage of workers. African Americans were eager to leave the South because of Jim Crow laws that led to mistreatment and violence against them. Many were sharecroppers who had difficulty surviving economically, especially when an insect **infestation** decimated the cotton crop during the war. Harlem also attracted black immigrants from the Caribbean, promising greater prosperity and economic opportunity. These movements of people

Literary Focus: The Harlem Renaissance

to large cities were part of a larger trend; in 1920, for the first time in U.S. history, more people lived in urban areas than in rural areas.

An unidentified woman, dressed in a fur-trimmed coat, posing in front of a tree on a Harlem sidewalk, 1920s

A Flowering of the Arts

5   In 1917, playwright Ridgely Torrence's *Three Plays for a Negro Theatre*, often considered among the first major works of the Harlem Renaissance, premiered. The suite of plays featured African-American actors and represented complex characters. The work rejected racial **stereotypes** frequently portrayed in the theater previously. For example, one of the most popular forms of musical entertainment in the late 1800s had been minstrel shows. These shows, featuring white men wearing makeup that made them appear to be African American, consisted of comedy and musical numbers that portrayed African Americans as foolish and simpleminded. In the early 1900s, African American musical performers sought to create their own musical theater that gave a more accurate portrayal of African American life and moved away from stereotypes. Eubie Blake and Noble Sissle wrote a musical called *Shuffle Along* in 1921. It became the first hit Broadway musical written by African Americans.

6   What's more, music attracted people from all races and walks of life to Harlem's nightclubs. This music included the blues, which originated in the Deep South in the late 1800s. The blues grew out of African American spirituals and work songs as well as the music of Africa and folk music. Blues music featured trancelike rhythm and unusual scales and chords.

7   Another musical form, jazz, drew partly from the blues. It, too, was invented by African Americans in the South in the late 1800s. Jazz features **improvisation**, in which the musicians create music as they play rather than reading it from sheets of paper. Bandleaders such as Duke Ellington and performers such as Louis Armstrong created some of the greatest jazz of any era. Jazz was created by African Americans in New Orleans in the late 1800s and represented an integral part of African American culture. It became so popular in the 1920s that the decade is sometimes referred to as the Jazz Age.

Literary Focus: The Harlem Renaissance

8. At the **outset** of the Harlem Renaissance, as African American musicians flocked to Harlem for work in the popular nightclubs, other artists soon followed. African-American artists living in Harlem had the opportunity to be trained and mentored by famous artists and to attend top schools in other parts of New York City. Among the artists who took advantage of these opportunities were painter Aaron Douglas and sculptor Augusta Savage.

9. Rising literacy levels among African Americans in the late 1800s made it possible for African Americans to consider writing as an occupation. Prior to the Civil War, few Southern African Americans could read because it was illegal to give instruction to enslaved persons. The growth of schools in the South for African Americans after the war meant that, when the Great Migration occurred, there was a burgeoning demand for literature and news by and about African Americans. The creation of African-American newspapers and magazines helped meet this need.

10. Among the most important magazines read by people in Harlem were *The Crisis* and *Opportunity: A Journal of Negro Life*. *The Crisis* was published by the National Association for the Advancement of Colored People (NAACP), an organization founded in New York City in 1909. The editor of *The Crisis* was W.E.B. Du Bois, who used the magazine to shed light on the oppression of African Americans and call for increased civil rights. Du Bois, a sociologist, was the leading activist for African Americans during the early 1900s. He appointed Jessie Fauset as literary editor of *The Crisis*. She published works by most of Harlem's leading authors. Another important group of African-American activists, the National Urban League, published *Opportunity*. This journal published, in addition to literature, studies of the difficulties faced by African Americans, including discrimination.

Political Activism Voices of Change

11. At the **outset** of the Harlem Renaissance, Marcus Garvey launched one of the largest mass movements in African American history. Garvey, who had emigrated from Jamaica in 1916, led the Universal Negro Improvement Association. A charismatic speaker, Garvey urged African Americans to become economically strong and suggested that they help form a black-led nation in Africa. He published a newspaper called *Negro World* that ran stories describing achievements of African Americans as well as features about African culture. At its peak his movement had over one million followers. While his ideas could be divisive among members of the Harlem Renaissance movement, his work influenced contemporary political thinking.

12. One of the most widely talented figures in the Harlem Renaissance was James Weldon Johnson. After serving as a **diplomat** to South American countries under President Theodore Roosevelt, Johnson became the first African American to serve as executive secretary of the NAACP. He had

Literary Focus: The Harlem Renaissance

distinguished himself within the organization for his campaign against lynching. As leader of the NAACP, he helped to expand the organization and fight limitations on voting rights in the South. Johnson was also talented in poetry and music. He served as a mentor to young poets and collected their work in important anthologies. He and his brother wrote the song "Lift Every Voice and Sing," sometimes referred to today as the Black National Anthem.

Writer and educator James Weldon Johnson (1871–1938) was one of the founders of the NAACP and served as the group's secretary from 1916 to 1930.

Major Concepts

- **End Stereotypes**—At the time of the Harlem Renaissance, many white people regarded African Americans as not being deserving of equal rights. Negative portrayals of African Americans extended beyond just minstrel shows and could also be found in fiction and motion pictures created by whites. African-American authors worked to **dispel** these images in two ways. First, they portrayed the diversity of African Americans, describing lives in many types of settings. Second, the quality of the literary output of these writers provided strong evidence that they were fully deserving of equal education and equal rights.

- **Protest Oppression**—Harlem writers worked to create a historical record of the injustices endured by African Americans. Lynchings, race riots, and other mob violence were epidemic throughout the period of the Harlem Renaissance. Harlem writers also drew attention to segregation and denials of constitutional rights. Discrimination in all its forms was another important topic.

- **Experiment with Modernism**—The mass slaughter of World War I led many artists to question the traditional beliefs of society. Writers in both Europe and the United States made a break with traditional literary forms and began to experiment. Individuals felt free to explore their own identities and imaginations. Modernist tropes were employed by many Harlem Renaissance writers, such as Jean Toomer's famous engagement with the movement in his novel *Cane* (1923).

Literary Focus: The Harlem Renaissance

- **Preserve Heritage**—Many writers who had migrated from the South wrote important works about their experiences there. They wrote about both the positive aspects of African American communities and the negative experiences of persecution by whites. Another important aspect of preserving heritage was writing about Africa. For example, Countee Cullen explored African themes in some of his finest poetry.

- **Everyday Themes**—As part of the effort to combat stereotypes, African American writers in Harlem sought to define and celebrate the common activities of African Americans. An important novel about working-class African Americans was Zora Neale Hurston's *Their Eyes Were Watching God*, which includes elements of magical realism. Poets of the Harlem Renaissance often wrote about challenges common among many African Americans. Claude McKay's "If We Must Die" is a powerful indictment of white violence against African Americans. In Arna Bontemps's "A Black Man Talks of Reaping," the speaker's memories of the anxiety of farming lead to thoughts about the difficulties faced by the next generation.

Style and Form

Influence of Blues and Jazz

- Jazz and blues strongly influenced the writing style of authors of fiction and poetry during the Harlem Renaissance. It was evident in such literary techniques as rhythm and stream of consciousness, which sometimes mirrored improvised music in style. Such techniques lent a strong Modernist feel to compositions.

- Langston Hughes, one of the leading poets of the twentieth century, spoke about the influence of music on his work. "To me, jazz is a montage of a dream deferred. A great big dream—yet to come—and always *yet*—to become ultimately and finally true." The influence of blues is also evident in Hughes's work. His poem "The Weary Blues" concerns a blues singer and begins,

   > Droning a drowsy syncopated tune,
   > Rocking back and forth to a mellow croon

Blending the Traditional with the Modern

- Although Harlem Renaissance writers experimented with Modernist forms, there was a strong traditional streak in their work as well. Zora Neale Hurston collected folklore and oral histories from African Americans in the South while she was a college student. Then she moved to Harlem and drew on this research to create satires and other literary forms. Poets, including Countee Cullen and Claude McKay, used traditional forms such as sonnets to frame their Modernist themes.

- Alain Locke, a professor of philosophy at Howard University, urged Harlem artists to draw on African history and subjects in their work. Locke collected the work of top Harlem writers in *The New Negro*. This anthology showed the diversity of the African-American experience, which was another way of combating the stereotypes that had grown up around portrayals of African Americans in prior decades.

16. The Great Depression is often considered the moment of the Harlem Renaissance's decline, as many African Americans left Harlem in search of jobs elsewhere. The rich artistic output of Harlem's artists would endure, however. Today, a line can be drawn connecting Harlem Renaissance writers and musicians to poets of the Black Arts Movement in the 1960s, such as Amiri Baraka and Nikki Giovanni, and to hip hop artists, like Kendrick Lamar. The Harlem Renaissance was an artistic movement that brought the social, political, and cultural realities of urban African-American life to mainstream culture and remains widely influential today. How do artists of the Harlem Renaissance continue to inspire music and culture today?

Literary Focus

Read "Literary Focus: The Harlem Renaissance." After you read, complete the Think Questions below.

THINK QUESTIONS

1. What caused the Great Migration of African Americans from the South to large Northern cities? Cite textual evidence to support your answer.

2. How did the NAACP play an important role in the Harlem Renaissance?

3. How did Harlem Renaissance writers make a break with the traditions of American literature from previous eras? Support your answer with evidence from the text.

4. The word *stereotype* comes from the Greek *stereos*, meaning "solid" and the Latin *typus,* meaning "image." With this information in mind and using context clues, write your best definition of the word **stereotype** as it used in this text. Cite any words or phrases that were particularly helpful in coming to your conclusion.

5. Use context clues to determine the meaning of the word **improvisation**. Write your best definition here, along with the words and phrases that were most helpful in determining the word's meaning. Then, check a dictionary to confirm your understanding.

The Negro Speaks of Rivers

POETRY
Langston Hughes
1921

Introduction

One of American literature's most distinguished and innovative writers, Langston Hughes (1902–1967) was a prominent figure of the Harlem Renaissance in the early half of the 20th century. "The Negro Speaks of Rivers" was first published in *The Crisis*, the official magazine of the National Association for the Advancement of Colored People, or NAACP—edited at the time by W.E.B. Du Bois—when Hughes was just 20 years old. The poem remains one of Hughes's most famous. It is a stirring exploration of race and the human past, seen through the timeless and symbolic lens of the world's ancient rivers.

"My soul has grown deep like the rivers."

1 I've known rivers:
2 I've known rivers **ancient** as the world and older than the
3   flow of human blood in human veins.

4 My soul has grown deep like the rivers.

5 I bathed in the Euphrates[1] when dawns were young.
6 I built my hut near the Congo and it **lulled** me to sleep.
7 I looked upon the Nile and raised the pyramids above it.
8 I heard the singing of the Mississippi when Abe Lincoln
9   went down to New Orleans[2], and I've seen its muddy
10   **bosom** turn all golden in the sunset.

11 I've known rivers:
12 Ancient, **dusky** rivers.

13 My soul has grown deep like the rivers.

American poet and writer *Langston Hughes* (1902 - 1967), circa 1945

---

1. **Euphrates** a river that flows from eastern Turkey through Syria and Iraq, bordering what was once Mesopotamia, the birthplace of human civilization
2. **Abe Lincoln / went down to New Orleans** When he was young, Abraham Lincoln twice sailed down the Mississippi River to New Orleans, his first exposure to the magnitude of the slave trade in 19th-century America.

WRITE

POETRY: Langston Hughes composed this poem when he had just graduated from high school, at the age of 17, while crossing the Mississippi River by train outside his hometown of St. Louis, Missouri. He was inspired by what he saw and by his relationship to the landscape and its history. Think about a view that inspires you. Imagine that you are looking out a particular window, at a particular landscape. Now write a poem about what you see and how it influences your sense of self and place. The landscape can be real or imagined, but should be one to which you feel a connection. In your poem, mimic Hughes's use of repetition, historical and geographical references, and first-person point of view.

How It Feels to Be Colored Me

INFORMATIONAL TEXT
Zora Neale Hurston
1928

Introduction

Zora Neale Hurston (1891–1960) was an African American writer and anthropologist who was one of the leading voices in the Harlem Renaissance. Although Hurston's preacher father sometimes sought to "squinch" her spirit, her mother urged young Zora and her seven siblings to "jump at de sun," and jump she did. Ten years before the publication of her most famous novel, *Their Eyes Were Watching God*, Hurston made her own declaration of independence with the autobiographical essay presented here, "How It Feels to Be Colored Me."

"I remember the very day that I became colored."

NOTES

1   I am colored but I offer nothing in the way of extenuating circumstances except the fact that I am the only Negro in the United States whose grandfather on the mother's side was *not* an Indian chief.

2   I remember the very day that I became colored. Up to my thirteenth year I lived in the little Negro town of Eatonville, Florida. It is exclusively a colored town. The only white people I knew passed through the town going to or coming from Orlando. The native whites rode dusty horses, the Northern tourists chugged down the sandy village road in automobiles. The town knew the Southerners and never stopped cane chewing when they passed. But the Northerners were something else again. They were peered at cautiously from behind curtains by the timid. The more venturesome would come out on the porch to watch them go past and got just as much pleasure out of the tourists as the tourists got out of the village.

3   The front porch might seem a daring place for the rest of the town, but it was a gallery seat for me. My favorite place was atop the gatepost. Proscenium box for a born first-nighter. Not only did I enjoy the show, but I didn't mind the actors knowing that I liked it. I usually spoke to them in passing. I'd wave at them and when they returned my salute, I would say something like this: "Howdy-do-well-I-thank-you-where-you-goin'?" Usually automobile or the horse paused at this, and after a queer exchange of compliments, I would probably "go a piece of the way" with them, as we say in farthest Florida. If one of my family happened to come to the front in time to see me, of course negotiations would be rudely broken off. But even so, it is clear that I was the first "welcome-to-our-state" Floridian, and I hope the Miami Chamber of Commerce will please take notice.

4   During this period, white people differed from colored to me only in that they rode through town and never lived there. They liked to hear me "speak pieces" and sing and wanted to see me dance the parse-me-la, and gave me generously of their small silver for doing these things, which seemed strange to me for I wanted to do them so much that I needed **bribing** to stop, only they didn't know it. The colored people gave no dimes. They **deplored** any

Skill: Author's Purpose and Point of View

Hurston explains that when she was a child white people treated her as if she existed for their entertainment. She wants to inform readers that, though African Americans didn't give her money, they gave her a place to belong.

joyful tendencies in me, but I was their Zora nevertheless. I belonged to them, to the nearby hotels, to the county—everybody's Zora.

5 But changes came in the family when I was thirteen, and I was sent to school in Jacksonville. I left Eatonville, the town of the oleanders, a Zora. When I disembarked from the river-boat at Jacksonville, she was no more. It seemed that I had suffered a sea change. I was not Zora of Orange County any more, I was now a little colored girl. I found it out in certain ways. In my heart as well as in the mirror, I became a fast brown—warranted not to rub nor run.

6 But I am not tragically colored. There is no great sorrow dammed up in my soul, nor lurking behind my eyes. I do not mind at all. I do not belong to the sobbing school of Negrohood who hold that nature somehow has given them a lowdown dirty deal and whose feelings are all but about it. Even in the helter-skelter[1] skirmish that is my life, I have seen that the world is to the strong regardless of a little pigmentation more or less. No, I do not weep at the world—I am too busy sharpening my oyster knife.

7 Someone is always at my elbow reminding me that I am the granddaughter of slaves. It fails to register **depression** with me. Slavery is sixty years in the past. The operation was successful and the patient is doing well, thank you. The terrible struggle that made me an American out of a potential slave said "On the line!" The Reconstruction said "Get set!" and the generation before said "Go!" I am off to a flying start and I must not halt in the stretch to look behind and weep. Slavery is the price I paid for civilization, and the choice was not with me. It is a bully adventure and worth all that I have paid through my ancestors for it. No one on earth ever had a greater chance for glory. The world to be won and nothing to be lost. It is thrilling to think—to know that for any act of mine, I shall get twice as much praise or twice as much blame. It is quite exciting to hold the center of the national stage, with the spectators not knowing whether to laugh or to weep.

8 The position of my white neighbor is much more difficult. No brown specter pulls up a chair beside me when I sit down to eat. No dark ghost thrusts its leg against mine in bed. The game of keeping what one has is never so exciting as the game of getting.

9 I do not always feel colored. Even now I often achieve the unconscious Zora of Eatonville before the Hegira.[2] I feel most colored when I am thrown against a sharp white background.

---

1. **helter-skelter** in a disorderly or hasty manner
2. **Hegira** the journey of Muhammad and his followers from Mecca to Medina in the 7th century

Skill: Figurative Language

This use of hyperbole emphasizes the author's enthusiasm and optimism at this point in her life. Again she uses a stage metaphor, but now she describes herself as being on center stage with the world as her audience.

Skill: Central or Main Idea

As an adult, the author is now more aware of her race. She feels like a dark rock, surrounded by white people. She feels her race and how it impacts who she is, but she is still able to be herself. Her race does not define her.

10   For instance at Barnard.[3] "Beside the waters of the Hudson" I feel my race. Among the thousand white persons, I am a dark rock surged upon, and overswept, but through it all, I remain myself. When covered by the waters, I am; and the ebb but reveals me again.

11   Sometimes it is the other way around. A white person is set down in our midst, but the contrast is just as sharp for me. For instance, when I sit in the drafty basement that is The New World Cabaret with a white person, my color comes. We enter chatting about any little nothing that we have in common and are seated by the jazz waiters. In the abrupt way that jazz orchestras have, this one plunges into a number. It loses no time in **circumlocutions,** but gets right down to business. It constricts the thorax and splits the heart with its tempo and narcotic harmonies. This orchestra grows rambunctious, rears on its hind legs and attacks the tonal veil with primitive fury, rending it, clawing it until it breaks through to the jungle beyond. I follow those heathen—follow them exultingly. I dance wildly inside myself; I yell within, I whoop; I shake my assegai above my head, I hurl it true to the mark *yeeeeooww*! I am in the jungle and living in the jungle way. My face is painted red and yellow and my body is painted blue. My pulse is throbbing like a war drum. I want to slaughter something—give pain, give death to what, I do not know. But the piece ends. The men of the orchestra wipe their lips and rest their fingers. I creep back slowly to the veneer we call civilization with the last tone and find the white friend sitting motionless in his seat, smoking calmly.

12   "Good music they have here," he remarks, drumming the table with his fingertips.

13   Music. The great blobs of purple and red emotion have not touched him. He has only heard what I felt. He is far away and I see him but dimly across the ocean and the continent that have fallen between us. He is so pale with his whiteness then and I am *so* colored.

14   At certain times I have no race, I am *me*. When I set my hat at a certain angle and saunter down Seventh Avenue, Harlem City, feeling as snooty as the lions in front of the Forty-Second Street Library, for instance. So far as my feelings are concerned, Peggy Hopkins Joyce[4] on the Boule Mich with her gorgeous raiment, stately carriage, knees knocking together in a most aristocratic manner, has nothing on me. The cosmic Zora emerges. I belong to no race nor time. I am the eternal feminine with its string of beads.

---

3. **Barnard** a liberal arts college in New York City
4. **Peggy Hopkins Joyce** an American model and actress known for leading a flamboyant, decadent lifestyle

15 I have no separate feeling about being an American citizen and colored. I am merely a fragment of the Great Soul that surges within the boundaries. My country, right or wrong.

16 Sometimes, I feel discriminated against, but it does not make me angry. It merely astonishes me. How *can* any deny themselves the pleasure of my company? It's beyond me.

17 But in the main, I feel like a brown bag of **miscellany** propped against a wall. Against a wall in company with other bags, white, red and yellow. Pour out the contents, and there is discovered a jumble of small things priceless and worthless. A first-water diamond, an empty spool, bits of broken glass, lengths of string, a key to a door long since crumbled away, a rusty knife-blade, old shoes saved for a road that never was and never will be, a nail bent under the weight of things too heavy for any nail, a dried flower or two still a little fragrant. In your hand is the brown bag. On the ground before you is the jumble it held—so much like the jumble in the bags, could they be emptied, that all might be dumped in a single heap and the bags refilled without altering the content of any greatly. A bit of colored glass more or less would not matter. Perhaps that is how the Great Stuffer of Bags filled them in the first place—who knows?

"How It Feels to Be Colored Me" from *I Love Myself When I Am Laughing* by Zora Neale Hurston. Published by The Feminist Press. Used by permission of The Permissions Company, Inc.

How It Feels to Be Colored Me

First Read

Read "How It Feels to Be Colored Me." After you read, complete the Think Questions below.

THINK QUESTIONS

1. How is life in Jacksonville different for Zora to the way it was in Eatonville? What are the significant changes, and how do they affect her? Cite evidence from the text to support your answer.

2. Why doesn't being the granddaughter of slaves "register depression" in Zora? Summarize Hurston's position on this part of her cultural history, quoting passages from the text to support your response.

3. What does Hurston's anecdote about The New World Cabaret convey to readers? Why does she share this story? Use evidence from the text to support your response.

4. What does the verb **deplored** mean as it appears in the text? Write your best definition of *deplored* here, along with a brief explanation of how you arrived at its meaning.

5. The Latin root *circum* means "around." With this in mind, what context clues helped you determine the meaning of **circumlocutions** as it appears in the text?

Skill:
Central or Main Idea

Use the Checklist to analyze Central or Main Idea in "How It Feels to Be Colored Me." Refer to the sample student annotations about Central or Main Idea in the text.

••• CHECKLIST FOR CENTRAL OR MAIN IDEA

In order to identify two or more central ideas of a text, note the following:

- ✓ the main idea in each paragraph or group of paragraphs
- ✓ key details in each paragraph or section of text, distinguishing what they have in common
- ✓ whether the details contain information that could indicate more than one main idea in a text
    - a science text, for example, may provide information about a specific environment and also a message on ecological awareness
    - a biography may contain equally important ideas about a person's achievements, influence, and the time period in which the person lives or lived
- ✓ when each central idea emerges
- ✓ ways that the central ideas interact and build on one another

To determine two or more central ideas of a text and analyze their development over the course of the text, including how they interact and build on one another to provide a complex analysis, consider the following questions:

- ✓ What main idea(s) do the details in each paragraphs explain or describe?
- ✓ What central or main ideas do all the paragraphs support?
- ✓ How do the central ideas interact with and build on one another? How does that affect when they emerge?
- ✓ How might you provide an objective summary of the text? What details would you include?

How It Feels to Be Colored Me

Skill:
Central or Main Idea

Reread paragraphs 15–17 of "How It Feels to Be Colored Me." Then, using the Checklist on the previous page, answer the multiple-choice questions below.

YOUR TURN

1. This question has two parts. First, answer Part A. Then, answer Part B.

    Part A: What is the main idea of the final paragraph of the essay?

    ○ A. Despite differing appearances on the exterior, all human beings are quite similar on the inside.
    ○ B. The author does not feel threatened by people of other races.
    ○ C. It does not matter what color you are because all human beings are worthy of respect.
    ○ D. There are many random things that make us who we are.

    Part B: Which line from the passage provides the best evidence to your answer in Part A?

    ○ A. ". . . old shoes saved for a road that never was and never will be, a nail bent under the weight of things too heavy for any nail, a dried flower or two still a little fragrant."
    ○ B. "Against a wall in company with other bags, white, red and yellow."
    ○ C. "Pour out the contents, and there is discovered a jumble of small things priceless and worthless."
    ○ D. ". . . could they be emptied, that all might be dumped in a single heap and the bags refilled without altering the content of any greatly."

Skill: Figurative Language

Use the Checklist to analyze Figurative Language in "How It Feels to Be Colored Me." Refer to the sample student annotations about Figurative Language in the text.

••• CHECKLIST FOR FIGURATIVE LANGUAGE

In order to determine the meaning of figurative language in context, note the following:

- ✓ words that mean one thing literally and suggest something else
- ✓ figures of speech, including metaphors and similes
- ✓ figures of speech, including hyperbole, or exaggerated statements not meant to be taken literally, such as:
  - a child saying "I'll be doing this homework until I'm 100!"
  - a claim such as, "I'm so hungry I could eat a horse!"

In order to interpret figurative language in context and analyze its role in the text, consider the following questions:

- ✓ Where is there figurative language in the text, and what seems to be the purpose of the author's use of it?
- ✓ Why does the author use a figure of speech rather than literal language?
- ✓ What impact do similes, metaphors, or hyperbole have on your understanding of the text?
- ✓ How does the figurative language develop the message or theme of the text?

How It Feels to Be Colored Me

Skill: Figurative Language

Reread paragraph 11 of "How It Feels to Be Colored Me." Then, using the Checklist on the previous page, answer the multiple-choice questions below.

YOUR TURN

1. Figurative language such as "rears on its hind legs" and "throbbing like a war drum" suggest what about the author's reaction to the music?

   - A. The figurative language shows that the music makes the author very anxious.
   - B. The figurative language shows that the author very much dislikes the music.
   - C. The figurative language shows that the music brings out something animalistic in the author.
   - D. The figurative language shows that different people have different reactions to music.

2. What is the intended effect of the author's hyperbolic descriptions of her actions while listening to the music?

   - A. They intend to illustrate the stark contrast between her reaction to the music and that of her white companion.
   - B. They intend to illustrate the intense personal connection that the author has to jazz music because of where she comes from.
   - C. They intend to illustrate how negative a reaction the author has to the music.
   - D. They intend to illustrate for the reader how music plays an important role in the author's adult life.

Skill: Author's Purpose and Point of View

Use the Checklist to analyze Author's Purpose and Point of View in "How It Feels to Be Colored Me." Refer to the sample student annotations about Author's Purpose and Point of View in the text.

••• CHECKLIST FOR AUTHOR'S PURPOSE AND POINT OF VIEW

In order to identify author's purpose and point of view, note the following:

- ✓ whether the writer is attempting to establish trust by citing his or her experience or education
- ✓ whether the evidence the author provides is convincing and that the argument or position is logical
- ✓ what words and phrases the author uses to appeal to the emotions
- ✓ the author's use of rhetoric, or the art of speaking and writing persuasively, such as the use of repetition to drive home a point, as well as allusion and alliteration
- ✓ the author's use of rhetoric to contribute to the power, persuasiveness, or beauty of the text

To determine the author's purpose and point of view, consider the following questions:

- ✓ How does the author try to convince me that he or she has something valid and important for me to read?
- ✓ What words or phrases express emotion or invite an emotional response? How or why are they effective or ineffective?
- ✓ What words and phrases contribute to the power, persuasiveness, or beauty of the text? Is the author's use of rhetoric successful? Why or why not?

Skill: Author's Purpose and Point of View

Reread paragraph 17 of "How It Feels to Be Colored Me." Then, using the Checklist on the previous page, answer the multiple-choice questions below.

YOUR TURN

1. Which of the following sentences **best** describes the purpose the author wants to achieve regarding her audience in this paragraph?

   - A. Hurston wants her audience to recognize that their lives are random and simplistic.
   - B. Hurston wants to show her audience that individual lives are just a random jumble of ideas that mean very little.
   - C. Hurston wants to persuade her audience to see that we're all similar on the inside and that is what matters.
   - D. Hurston wants the audience to share her view that every object in the world is "a fragment of the Great Soul."

2. What point of view is the author imparting in this passage?

   - A. Racism is the result of economic injustice.
   - B. People should share and then redistribute their wealth.
   - C. Race is not an indicator of worth or value.
   - D. People who are alike on the inside get mistreated because of race.

Close Read

Reread "How It Feels to Be Colored Me" and "The Negro Speaks of Rivers." As you reread, complete the Skills Focus questions below. Then use your answers and annotations from the questions to help you complete the Write activity.

SKILLS FOCUS

1. Analyze context, including imagery, to help you determine the nuanced meaning of the word *fast* in paragraph 5. Explain how context clues helped you understand the word's meaning.

2. Highlight an example of how Hurston uses figurative language. Explain how such rhetorical devices affect your reading experience and your understanding the text.

3. Identify an example in which Hurston seems to be encouraging herself to stand strong against the tide of racial difference. What main idea is she communicating to the reader? Analyze how addressing a dual audience deepens the meaning of the text.

4. Find an example of when Hurston feels least confined by perceptions of race as an adult. Analyze how the author's description of herself in this example relates to her purpose and point of view.

5. How might Hurston's outlook on her identity have been different if she had never left home? Highlight evidence from the text to support your answer.

WRITE

DISCUSSION: How do Hurston and Hughes each use figurative language to convey the central ideas of their texts? Determine the central idea or ideas of each text and evaluate how well the author conveys these ideas. Then, describe to what extent figurative language strengthens central ideas, using relevant evidence from the text.

Fences

DRAMA
August Wilson
1985

Introduction

Fences is a Pulitzer Prize-winning play by August Wilson (1945–2005), one of his ten plays collectively referred to as "The Pittsburgh Cycle." Each play in the cycle focuses on the African American experience during a particular decade in 20th-century America; though it premiered in 1985, Fences is set in the latter half of the 1950s. In this scene, Cory, a high school senior, confronts his father, a garbage collector and former Negro League baseball player named Troy, about pursuing a future in college football. The ensuing argument escalates quickly, and despite Cory's mother Rose's interruption, Troy lands several verbal blows.

"I'm the boss around here. I do the only saying that counts."

> *Note: The text you are about to read contains offensive language. Remember to be mindful of the thoughts and feelings of your peers as you read and discuss this text. Please consult your teacher for additional guidance and support.*

1 Troy: Where's Cory? That boy brought his butt home yet?

2 Rose: He's in the house doing chores. *(calling)* Cory! Get your butt out here, boy!
(Troy goes over to a pile of wood, picks up a board, and starts sawing. Cory enters from the house.)

3 Troy: You just now coming in here from leaving this morning?

4 Cory: Yeah, I had to go to football practice.

5 Troy: Yeah, what?

6 Cory: Yessir.

7 Troy: I ain't but two seconds off you noway. The garbage sitting in there overflowing . . . you ain't done none of your chores . . . and you come in here talking about "Yeah."

8 Cory: I was just getting ready to do my chores now, pop . . .

9 Troy: Your first chore is to help me with this fence on Saturday. Everything else come after that. Now get that saw and cut them boards.

10 *(Cory begins to get out the boards. There's a long pause.)*

11 Troy: Your mama told me you done got **recruited** by a college football team? Is that right?

12 Cory: Yeah, Coach Zellman say the recruiter gonna be coming by to talk to you. Get you to sign the permission papers.

13 Troy: I thought you supposed to be working down there at the A&P. Ain't you supposed to be working down there after school?

Skill: Dramatic Elements and Structure

Troy is agitated and starts sawing boards, which seems menacing and tense. Cory enters the scene from the house. His dismissive "yeah" response upsets Troy even more. Troy demands he say "yessir" suggesting he expects respect.

Fences

14 Cory: Mr. Stawicki say he gonna hold my job for me until after the football season. Say starting next week I can work weekends.

15 Troy: I thought we had an understanding about this football stuff? You supposed to keep up with your chores and hold that job down at the A&P. Ain't been around here all Saturday. Ain't none of your chores done . . . now you telling me you done quit your job.

16 Cory: I'm gonna be working weekends.

17 Troy: You damn right you are! And ain't no need for nobody coming around here to talk to me about signing for nothing.

18 Cory: Hey pop . . . you can't do that. He coming all the way from North Carolina.

19 Troy: I don't care where he coming from. The white man ain't gonna let you nowhere with that football noway. You go on and get your book-learning so you can work yourself up in that A&P or learn how to fix cars or build houses or something, get you a **trade**. That way you have something can't nobody take away from you. You go on and learn how to put your hands to some good use. Besides **hauling** people's garbage.

20 Cory: I get good grades, Pop. That's why the recruiter wants to talk with you. You got to keep up your grades to get recruited. This way I'll be going to college. I'll get a chance.

Skill: Summarizing

Without telling his father, Cory quits his job. Troy finds out after the fact, tells Cory to get his job back, finds out it isn't available, and insists Cory get another job.

21 Troy: First you gonna get your butt down there to the A&P and get your job back.

22 Cory: Mr. Stawicki done already hired somebody else 'cause I told him I was playing football.

23 Troy: You a bigger fool than I thought . . . to let somebody take away your job so you can play some football. Where you gonna get your money to take out your girlfriend and whatnot? What kind of foolishness is that to let somebody take away your job?

24 Cory: I'm still gonna be working weekends.

25 Troy: Naw . . . naw. You getting your butt out of here and finding another job.

26 Cory: Come on pop! I got to practice. I can't work after school and play football too. The team needs me. That's what Coach Zellman say . . .

27 Troy: I don't care what nobody else say, I'm the boss . . . you understand? I'm the boss around here. I do the only saying that counts.

28 Cory: Come on, pop!

29 Troy: I asked you . . . did you understand?

30 Cory: Yessir.

31 Troy: You go on down there to that A&P and see if you can get your job back. If you can't do both . . . then you quit the football team. You've got to take the crookeds with the straights.

32 Cory: Yessir.
    (Pause)
    . . . Can I ask you a question?

33 Troy: What the hell you wanna ask me? Mr. Stawicki the one you got the questions for.

34 Cory: How come you ain't never liked me?

35 Troy: Liked you? Who the hell say I got to like you? What law is there say I got to like you? Wanna stand up in my face and ask a damn fool ass question like that. Talking about liking somebody. Come here boy, when I talk to you . . . Straighten up dammit! I asked you a question . . . what law is there say I got to like you?

36 Cory: None.

37 Troy: Well, all right then! Don't you eat every day? *(Pause)* Answer me when I talk to you! Don't you eat every day?

38 Cory: Yeah.

39 Troy: N-----, as long as you in my house, you put that sir on the end of it when you talk to me!

40 Cory: Yes . . . sir.

41 Troy: You eat every day.

42 Cory: Yessir!

43 Troy: You got clothes on your back.

44 Cory: Yessir.

45 Troy: Why you think that is?

46 Cory: Cause of you.

47 Troy: Ah, hell I know it's cause of me . . . but why do you think that is?

48 Cory **(hesitant)**: Cause you like me.

Skill: Dramatic Elements and Structure

Troy wants Cory to keep the job and quit the team. I think Troy's message about the "crookeds and straights" is about taking the good with the bad. Cory's pause implies he disagrees but is hesitant to further anger Troy.

49 Troy: Like you? I go out of here every morning . . . bust my butt putting up with them crackers everyday . . . 'cause I like you? You about the biggest fool I ever saw. *(Pause)* It's my job, it's my responsibility! You understand that? A man got to take care of his family. You live in my house, sleep on my bedclothes, fill your belly up on my food . . . cause you my son. You my flesh and blood. Not cause I like you! Cause it's my duty to take care of you. I owe a responsibility to you! Let's get this straight here, before it go along any further . . . I ain't got to like you. Mr. Rand don't give me my money come payday 'cause he likes me. He gives me 'cause he owes me. I done given you everything I had to give you. I gave you your life! Me and your mama worked that out between us. And liking your black ass wasn't part of the bargain. Don't you try and go through life worrying about if somebody like you or not. You best be making sure they doing right by you. You understand what I'm saying boy?

50 Cory: Yessir.

51 Troy: Then get the hell out of my face, and get on down to that A&P.

52 *(Rose has been standing behind the screen door for much of the scene. She enters as Cory exits.)*

53 Rose: Why don't you let the boy go ahead and play football Troy? Ain't no harm in that. He's just trying to be like you with the sports.

54 Troy: I don't want him to be like me! I want him to move as far away from my life as he can get. You the only decent thing that's ever happened to me. I wish him that. But I don't wish him a thing else from my life. I decided seventeen years ago that boy wasn't getting involved in no sports. Not after what they did to me.

55 Rose: Everything that boy do . . . he do it for you. He wants you to say "Good job, son." That's all.

56 Troy: Rose, I ain't got time for that. He's alive. He's healthy. He's got to make his own way. I made mine. Ain't nobody gonna hold his hand when he get out there in the real world.

57 Rose: Times have changed from when you was young, Troy. People change. The world is changing around you and you can't even see it.

58 Troy *(slow, **methodical**)*: Woman . . . I do the best I can do. I come home every Friday. I carry a sack of potatoes and a bucket of lard. You all line up at the door with your hands out. I give you the lint from my pockets. I give you my sweat and blood. I ain't got no tears. I done spent them. I get up on Monday morning . . . find my lunch on the table. I go out. Make my way. Find my strength to carry me through to the next Friday. *(Pause)* That's all I've got Rose. That's all I've got to give. I can't give nothing else.

Excerpted from *Fences* by August Wilson, published by Samuel French, Inc.

First Read

Read *Fences*. After you read, complete the Think Questions below.

THINK QUESTIONS

1. Cory answers "Yessir" to most of his father's statements. What can you infer about Cory's character based on his responses? Use evidence from the text to support your answer.

2. Troy says Rose is the "only decent thing that's ever happened" to him. Why does he say this? How would you describe Troy and Rose's relationship? Use evidence from the text to support your answer.

3. There are not many stage directions included in the text. How do you imagine Troy's tone of voice during this scene? Use evidence from the text to support your answer.

4. Read the following dictionary entry:

   trade
   trade /trād/ *noun*
   1. the action of buying and selling goods and services
   2. a skilled job
   3. an exchange between two people

   Decide which definition best matches **trade** as it is used in *Fences*. Write that definition of *trade* here, and indicate which clues found in the text helped you determine the meaning.

5. What is the meaning of the word **hauling** as it is used in paragraph 19 of *Fences*? Write your best definition here, along with a brief explanation of how you arrived at its meaning.

Skill: Dramatic Elements and Structure

Use the Checklist to analyze Dramatic Elements and Structure in *Fences*. Refer to the sample student annotations about Dramatic Elements and Structure in the text.

••• CHECKLIST FOR DRAMATIC ELEMENTS AND STRUCTURE

In order to determine the author's choices regarding the development of a drama, note the following:

- ✓ the names of all the characters, how they are introduced, and their relationships with one another
- ✓ character development, including personality traits, motivations, decisions they make, and actions they take
- ✓ the setting(s) of the story and how it influences the characters and the events of the plot
- ✓ how character choices and dialogue affect the plot
- ✓ the stage directions and how they are used to reveal character and plot development

To analyze the impact of the author's choices regarding how to develop and relate elements of a story or drama, consider the following questions:

- ✓ How does the order of events in the play affect the development of the drama?
- ✓ How are characters introduced, and what does it reveal about them?
- ✓ In what ways do the characters change over the course of the drama?
- ✓ How do the choices the characters make help advance the plot?
- ✓ How does the setting affect the characters and plot?
- ✓ How do the characters' actions help develop the theme or message of the play?

Skill: Dramatic Elements and Structure

Reread paragraphs 45–51 of *Fences*. Then, using the Checklist on the previous page, answer the multiple-choice questions below.

YOUR TURN

1. Based on the stage direction and dialogue between Troy and Cory in paragraphs 45 through 48, the reader can conclude that—

   - A. Troy and Cory feel at ease around each other.
   - B. Cory feels intimidated by his father's exertion of authority.
   - C. Both Troy and Cory have explosive personalities.
   - D. Cory is trying to apologize to Troy, but Troy is unwilling to listen to him.

2. The dialogue in paragraph 49 reveals that Troy—

   - A. supports his family out of love, even if he doesn't always show it.
   - B. likes and is proud of his job.
   - C. believes he has a duty to take care of Cory but that doesn't mean he has to like him.
   - D. wants to protect Cory from hardships in life.

3. The dramatic elements in this passage advance the plot in the overall scene by—

   - A. adding tension to the rising action.
   - B. providing a resolution to the conflict.
   - C. giving background information about Troy's past and how it influences his parenting style.
   - D. portraying the highest moment of tension, or climax, of the scene.

Fences

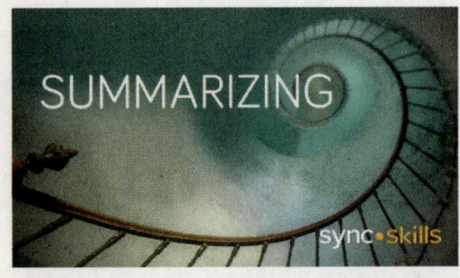

Skill: Summarizing

Use the Checklist to analyze Summarizing in *Fences*. Refer to the sample student annotations about Summarizing in the text.

••• CHECKLIST FOR SUMMARIZING

In order to determine how to write an objective summary of a text, consider the following:

- ✓ find details that answer the basic questions *who*, *what*, *where*, *when*, *why*, and *how*
- ✓ identify key details that support theme, plot, and other major story elements
- ✓ exclude from summaries minor details that don't contribute to the theme or plot
- ✓ exclude from summaries personal thoughts, judgments, or opinions to ensure that the summaries are objective

To provide an objective summary of a text, consider the following questions:

- ✓ What are the answers to basic *who*, *what*, *where*, *when*, *why*, and *how* questions?
- ✓ Have I included key details that support major story elements?
- ✓ Have I avoided including minor details that don't contribute to the theme or plot?
- ✓ Is my summary objective, or have I added my own thoughts, judgments, and personal opinions?

Skill: Summarizing

Reread paragraphs 52–56 of *Fences*. Then, using the Checklist on the previous page, answer the multiple-choice questions below.

YOUR TURN

1. This question has two parts. First, answer Part A. Then, answer Part B.

   Part A: Summarize how Troy feels about Cory playing college football.
   - A. Troy decided many years ago that Cory would not play sports in college because of the bad experience Troy had, which had a negative impact on his life.
   - B. Rose tries to convince Troy to allow Cory to play football by telling him that Cory wants to be like him.
   - C. Troy feels that playing football is too dangerous. Playing football in college could hurt Cory as it did Troy, and he does not want this for his son.
   - D. Troy does not want Cory to be at all like him because his life is miserable and because Cory needs to find his own way.

   Part B: What textual evidence best supports the correct answer to Part A?
   - A. "I don't want him to be like me! I want him to move as far away from my life as he can get."
   - B. "Why don't you let the boy go ahead and play football Troy? Ain't no harm in that."
   - C. "I decided seventeen years ago that boy wasn't getting involved in no sports. Not after what they did to me."
   - D. "Everything that boy do . . . he do it for you. He wants you to say 'Good job, son.' That's all."

2. Which statement provides the most objective summary of the information from this passage?

   - A. Cory storms off. Rose rushes in to tell Troy that all Cory wants is for Troy to show that he is proud of him by saying, "Good job, son." Troy agrees that he should do this.
   - B. Rose overhears Troy and Cory's conversation. She jumps to Cory's defense. She tells Troy that their son just wants to hear some encouragement from his father, that's all. Troy says he doesn't want his son to get involved in sports. Rose says Cory only wants to play sports because he wants to be like Troy.
   - C. Rose enters as Cory exits. Troy tells Rose that she is the best thing that's ever happened to him but he disagrees with her about Cory's future.
   - D. Rose tells Troy privately that Cory wants to be like Troy. Troy doesn't want Cory to be like him or to have the same bad experience with sports. Rose says Cory wants encouragement from Troy. Troy rebuffs her, explaining that Cory needs to learn the hard truths of the real world.

Close Read

Reread *Fences*. As you reread, complete the Skills Focus questions below. Then use your answers and annotations from the questions to help you complete the Write activity.

◎ SKILLS FOCUS

1. Locate lines at the beginning of the scene in which Troy demands that Cory address him formally and then asks Cory about being recruited. Explain how dramatic elements in this passage, such as dialogue and stage directions, work together to advance the plot.

2. Identify a paragraph in the middle of the play in which Troy insults Cory by calling him a fool. Analyze how the economic context of the setting influences Troy's characterization.

3. Identify evidence from the latter part of the play in which Troy discusses duty and responsibility. Based on this evidence, analyze how the economic context influences an important theme in the play.

4. Highlight the stage directions for Rose near the end of the scene, as well as the dialogue between Rose and Troy immediately following those stage directions. Objectively summarize the conflict occurring between Rose and Troy.

5. Highlight a section of the text in which Troy explains what it means to him to be a father. According to Troy, what is the relationship between a man and his home? What responsibilities does he have?

✎ WRITE

LITERARY ANALYSIS: Think about the setting and the action in this excerpt from *Fences*. How does the literal action—Troy constructing a fence in the backyard, and enlisting Cory to join him—coincide with what is happening in the dialogue? Analyze how the author uses dramatic elements and structure to develop the connection between literal action and the deeper relationship between the characters.

The Old Cabin

POETRY
Paul Laurence Dunbar
1905

Introduction

Paul Laurence Dunbar (1872–1906) was born and raised in Dayton, Ohio. His mother was a formerly enslaved person who learned how to read to support her son's education. Dunbar published poetry and fiction, as well as song lyrics for Broadway, and was one of the first African American poets to earn nationwide acclaim. As he does in this poem, Dunbar often experimented with writing in regional dialects along with conventional English. Dunbar expressed complicated feelings about writing in dialect. Although this dialect reflected his "natural speech," as he called it, he came to feel that writing in dialect biased white readers to African Americans. In this poem's original printing, "The Old Cabin" is accompanied by a series of black-and-white photographs depicting an African American woman in several scenes of life in slavery.

"I kin see de light a—shinin'"

1. In de dead of night I sometimes,
2. Git to t'inkin' of de pas'
3. An' de days w'en slavery helt me
4. In my mis'ry—ha'd an' fas'.
5. Dough de time was mighty tryin',
6. In dese houahs somehow hit seem
7. Dat a brightah light come slippin'
8. Thoo de kivahs of my dream.

9. An' my min' fu'gits de whuppins
10. Draps de feah o' block an' lash
11. An' flies straight to somep'n' joyful
12. In a secon's lightnin' flash.
13. Den hit seems I see a **vision**
14. Of a dearah long ago
15. Of de childern tumblin' roun' me
16. By my rough ol' cabin do'.

The Old Cabin

17 Talk about yo' go'geous mansions
18 An' yo' big house great an' gran',
19 Des bring up de fines' palace
20 Dat you know in all de lan'.
21 But dey's somep'n' dearah to me,
22 Somep'n' **faihah** to my eyes
23 In dat cabin, less you bring me
24 To yo' mansion in de skies.

25 I kin see de light a–shinin'
26 Thoo de chinks atween de logs,
27 I kin hyeah de way–off **bayin'**
28 Of my mastah's huntin' dogs,
29 An' de neighin' of de hosses
30 Stampin' on de ol' bahn flo',
31 But above dese soun's de laughin'
32 At my deah ol' cabin do'.

33 We would gethah daih at evenin',
34 All my frien's 'ud come erroun'
35 An' hit wan't no time, twell, bless you,

36 You could hyeah de banjo's soun'.
37 You could see de dahkies dancin'
38 Pigeon wing[1] an' heel an' toe—
39 Joyous times I tell you people
40 Roun' dat same ol' cabin do'.

41 But at times my t'oughts gits saddah,
42 Ez I **riccolec'** de folks,
43 An' dey **frolickin'** an' talkin'
44 Wid dey laughin' an dey jokes.
45 An' hit hu'ts me w'en I membahs
46 Dat I'll nevah see no mo'
47 Dem ah faces gethered smilin'
48 Roun' dat po' ol' cabin do'.

WRITE

RESEARCH Poetry written during the Harlem Renaissance incorporated specific themes and references pertaining to African American history and culture. Research this literary period. Then, write a literary analysis in which you investigate how "The Old Cabin"—written in 1905—prefigures some of the predominant themes and literary characteristics of the poetry of the Harlem Renaissance.

1. **Pigeon wing** an old-fashioned type of dance

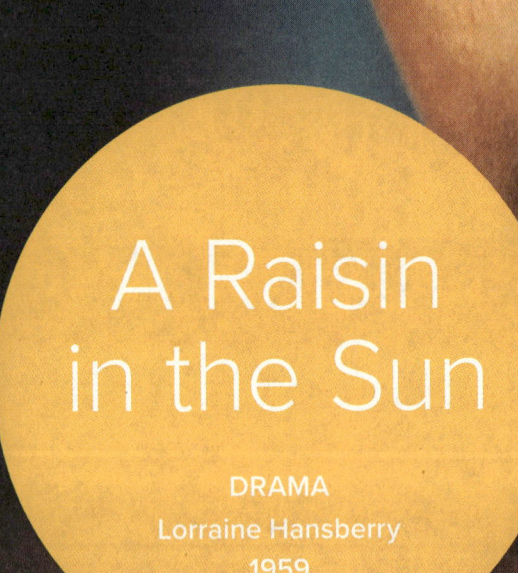

A Raisin in the Sun

DRAMA
Lorraine Hansberry
1959

Introduction

Set in the years after World War II, *A Raisin in the Sun* is an award-winning play by Lorraine Hansberry (1930–1965) about the Youngers, a fictional black family in Chicago struggling to keep things together during difficult financial times. In this excerpt from the third act of the play, son Walter has made a bad business decision and has lost the insurance money the family received from their father's death. He now comes up with a scheme to get some of the money back—but at what price?

"There is always something left to love. And if you ain't learned that you ain't learned nothing."

> Note: The text you are about to read contains offensive language. Remember to be mindful of the thoughts and feelings of your peers as you read and discuss this text. Please consult your teacher for additional guidance and support.

From Act III

1   RUTH: What did you call that man for, Walter Lee?

2   WALTER: Called him to tell him to come on over to the show. Gonna put on a show for the man. Just what he wants to see. You see, Mama, the man came here today and he told us that them people out there where you want us to move—well they so upset they willing to pay us not to move! *[He laughs.]* And—and oh, Mama you would have been proud of the way me and Ruth and Bennie acted. We told him to get out . . . . Lord have mercy! We told the man to get out! Oh, we was some proud folks this afternoon, yeah. *[He lights a cigarette.]* We were still full of that old-time stuff . . . .

3   RUTH (Walter's wife) *[coming toward him slowly]*: You talking 'bout taking them people's money to keep us from moving in that house?

4   WALTER: I ain't just talking 'bout it baby—I'm telling you that's what's going to happen!

5   BENEATHA (Walter's sister): Oh, God! Where is the bottom! Where is the real honest-to-God bottom so he can't go any farther!

6   WALTER: See—that's the old stuff. You and that boy was here today. You all want everybody to carry a flag and a spear and sing some marching songs, huh? You wanna spend your life looking into things and trying to find the right and wrong part, huh? Yeah. You know what's going to happen to that boy someday—he'll find himself sitting in a dungeon, locked in forever—and the takers will have the key! Forget it, baby! There ain't no causes—there ain't nothing but taking in this world, and he who takes most is smartest—and it don't make a damn bit of difference *how*.

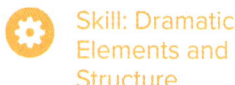

Skill: Dramatic Elements and Structure

Walter explains what happened earlier in the day, establishing context. Walter's behavior, relayed through stage directions, is flippant. Ruth's action and dialogue build tension, advancing the plot into the rising action.

A Raisin in the Sun

7   MAMA: You making something inside me cry, son. Some awful pain inside me.

8   WALTER: Don't cry, Mama. Understand. That white man is going to walk in that door able to write checks for more money than we ever had. It's important to him and I'm going to help him . . . I'm going to put on the show, Mama.

9   MAMA: Son—I come from five generations of people who was slaves and **sharecroppers**—but ain't nobody in my family never let nobody pay 'em no money that was a way of telling us we weren't fit to walk the earth. We ain't never been that poor. [*Raising her eyes and looking at him*] We ain't never been that—dead inside.

10 BENEATHA: Well—we are dead now. All the talk about dreams and sunlight that goes on in this house. It's all dead now.

11 WALTER: What's the matter with you all! I didn't make this world! It was give to me this way! Hell, yes, I want me some yachts someday! Yes, I want to hang some real pearls 'round my wife's neck. Ain't she supposed to wear no pearls? Somebody tell me—tell me, who decides which women is suppose to wear pearls in this world. I tell you I am a *man*—and I think my wife should wear some pearls in this world!

12 [*This last line hangs a good while and WALTER begins to move about the room. The word "Man" has penetrated his consciousness; he mumbles it to himself repeatedly between strange agitated pauses as he moves about.*]

13 MAMA: Baby, how you going to feel on the inside?

14 WALTER: Fine! . . . Going to feel fine . . . a man . . .

15 MAMA: You won't have nothing left then, Walter Lee.

16 WALTER [*coming to her*]: I'm going to feel fine, Mama. I'm going to look that son-of-a-bitch in the eyes and say—[*He falters.*]—and say, "All right, Mr. Lindner—[*He falters even more.*]—that's *your* neighborhood out there! You got the right to keep it like you want! You got the right to have it like you want! Just write the check and—the house is yours." And—and I am going to say—[*His voice almost breaks.*] "And you—you people just put the money in my hand and you won't have to live next to this bunch of stinking n------!"

17 . . . And maybe I'll just get down on my black knees . . . [*He does so,* RUTH *and* BENNIE *and* MAMA *watch him in frozen horror.*] "Captain, Mistuh, Bossman—[**groveling** *and grinning and wringing his hands in profoundly anguished imitation of the slow-witted movie stereotype*] Oh, yassuh boss! Yasssssuh! Great white—[*Voice breaking, he forces himself to go on.*]—Father, just gi' ussen de money, fo' God's sake, and we's—we's ain't gwine come out deh and dirty up yo' white folks neighborhood . . ." [*He breaks down completely.*] And I'll feel fine! Fine! FINE! [*He gets up and goes into the bedroom.*]

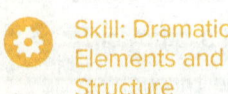

Skill: Dramatic Elements and Structure

Walter's words seem defiant, but the pauses and repetition in his speech, combined with the stage directions, undermine what he is saying. Walter's conscience is breaking through his rant, marking the beginning of the climax.

18 BENEATHA: That is not a man. That is nothing but a toothless rat.

19 MAMA: Yes—death done come in this here house. [*She is nodding, slowly,* **reflectively**.] Done come walking in my house on the lips of my children. You what supposed to be my beginning again. You—what supposed to be my harvest. [*to* BENEATHA] You—you mourning your brother?

20 BENEATHA: He's no brother of mine.

21 MAMA: What you say?

22 BENEATHA: I said that that individual in that room is no brother of mine.

23 MAMA: That's what I thought you said. You feeling like you better than he is today?

24 [BENEATHA *does not answer.*]

25 MAMA: Yes? What you tell him a minute ago? That he wasn't a man? Yes? You give him up for me? You done wrote his **epitaph** too—like the rest of the world? Well who give you the privilege?

26 BENEATHA: Be on my side for once! You saw what he just did, Mama! You saw him—down on his knees. Wasn't it you who taught me—to **despise** any man who would do that? Do what he's going to do?

27 MAMA: Yes—I taught you that. Me and your daddy. But I thought I taught you something else too . . . I thought I taught you to love him.

28 BENEATHA: Love him? There is nothing left to love.

29 MAMA: There is always something left to love. And if you ain't learned that you ain't learned nothing. [*looking at her*] Have you cried for that boy today? I don't mean for yourself and for the family 'cause we lost the money. I mean for him; what he been through and what it done to him. Child, when do you think is the time to love somebody the most; when they done good and made things easy for everybody? Well then, you ain't through learning—because that ain't the time at all. It's when he's at his lowest and can't believe in hisself 'cause the world done whipped him so! When you starts measuring somebody, measure him right, child, measure him right. Make sure you done taken into account what hills and valleys he come through before he got to wherever he is.

Excerpted from *A Raisin in the Sun* by Lorraine Hansberry, published by Vintage Books.

Skill:
Theme

The characters' dialogue in response to Walter's decision creates conflict. Mama reminds Beneatha about the value of unconditional love. This reveals one of the play's themes about the importance of family.

A Raisin in the Sun

First Read

Read *A Raisin in the Sun*. After you read, complete the Think Questions below.

 THINK QUESTIONS

1. Based on the text, what can you infer about Mr. Lindner's motivations for paying Walter and his family not to move?

2. How does Walter define manhood? Cite specific quotes or passages from the text to support your answer.

3. Why is Mama upset at Beneatha? Refer to specific moments in the text in your answer.

4. Use context to determine the meaning of the word **groveling** as it is used in *A Raisin in the Sun*. Write your definition of *groveling* here and explain how you arrived at it.

5. Use context to determine the meaning of the word **epitaph** as it is used in *A Raisin in the Sun*. Double check your answer using a dictionary. In your own words, write a definition of *epitaph* here.

A Raisin in the Sun

Skill: Dramatic Elements and Structure

Use the Checklist to analyze Dramatic Elements and Structure in *A Raisin in the Sun*. Refer to the sample student annotations about Dramatic Elements and Structure in the text.

••• CHECKLIST FOR DRAMATIC ELEMENTS AND STRUCTURE

In order to determine the author's choices regarding the development of a drama, note the following:

- ✓ the names of all the characters, how they are introduced, and their relationships with one another
- ✓ character development, including personality traits, motivations, decisions they make, and actions they take
- ✓ the setting(s) of the story and how it influences the characters and the events of the plot
- ✓ how characters' choices and dialogue affect the plot
- ✓ the stage directions and how they are used to reveal character and plot development

To analyze the impact of the author's choices regarding how to develop and relate elements of a story or drama, consider the following questions:

- ✓ How does the order of events in the play affect the development of the drama?
- ✓ How are characters introduced, and what does it reveal about them?
- ✓ In what ways do the characters change over the course of the drama?
- ✓ How do the choices the characters make help advance the plot?
- ✓ How does the setting affect the characters and plot?
- ✓ How do the characters' actions help develop the theme or message of the play?

A Raisin in the Sun

Skill: Dramatic Elements and Structure

Reread paragraph 17 of *A Raisin in the Sun*. Then, using the Checklist on the previous page, answer the multiple-choice questions below.

⟳ YOUR TURN

1. Which of the following sentences best describes the relationship between the dialogue and the stage directions in this passage?

   ○ A. The dialogue and the stage directions compliment each other to reinforce that Walter feels confident about his accepting the money from Mr. Lindner.

   ○ B. The aggressive mockery in the dialogue and the anguished horror of the stage directions reflect the extreme pain of Walter's conflict.

   ○ C. The dialogue and the stage directions work together to show that Ruth, Bennie, and Mama agree with Walter.

   ○ D. The painful dialogue and emotional stage directions show that the family is falling apart.

2. The relationship between the dialogue and the stage directions in this passage advance the plot by—

   ○ A. bringing the plot in this scene to its climax, or the point at which the conflict reaches its highest tension.

   ○ B. providing a resolution to the conflict.

   ○ C. giving background information, or exposition, about Walter's emotional state.

   ○ D. wrapping up loose ends in the falling action.

Skill: Theme

Use the Checklist to analyze Theme in *A Raisin in the Sun*. Refer to the sample student annotations about Theme in the text.

••• CHECKLIST FOR THEME

In order to identify two or more themes, or central ideas, of a text, note the following:

✓ the subject and how it relates to the themes in the text

✓ if one or more themes is stated directly in the text

✓ details in the text that help to reveal each theme:

- the title and chapter headings
- details about the setting
- the narrator's or speaker's tone
- characters' thoughts, actions, and dialogue
- the central conflict, climax, and resolution of the conflict
- shifts in characters, setting, or plot events

✓ when the themes interact with each other

To determine two or more themes, or central ideas, of a text and to analyze their development over the course of the text, including how they interact and build on one another to produce a complex account, consider the following questions:

✓ What are the themes in the text? When do they emerge?

✓ How does each theme develop over the course of the text?

✓ How do the themes interact and build on one another?

A Raisin in the Sun

Skill:
Theme

Reread paragraphs 9–15 of *A Raisin in the Sun*. Then, using the Checklist on the previous page, answer the multiple-choice questions below.

YOUR TURN

1. Which inference best demonstrates the relationship between characters and the theme about manhood as seen in paragraph 11?

   - A. Walter does not think sharecroppers are considered men.
   - B. Walter wants to win over his wife's affection by buying her pearls.
   - C. Walter acknowledges that all men want to own a yacht.
   - D. Walter prioritizes the expectation of proving his manhood by providing for his wife.

2. Beneatha's comments in paragraph 10 reveal that—

   - A. the characters live in a racially segregated neighborhood.
   - B. someone died in the house.
   - C. their home used to have a hopeful atmosphere.
   - D. there is no natural lighting in the house.

3. Which paragraph best communicates the message that being poor doesn't necessitate a loss of dignity and self-respect?

   - A. 9
   - B. 12
   - C. 13
   - D. 14

Close Read

Reread *A Raisin in the Sun*. As you reread, complete the Skills Focus questions below. Then use your answers and annotations from the questions to help you complete the Write activity.

SKILLS FOCUS

1. Highlight an exchange of dialogue between Beneatha and Walter that shows how Beneatha feels about the family's dreams and Walter's reaction. Analyze the relationship between plot and theme in these lines.

2. Identify a passage that includes dialogue and stage directions that show what Walter thinks it means to be a man. Analyze how these dramatic elements help advance the plot of the play.

3. Locate a passage that contains clues about the setting of *A Raisin in the Sun*. How does the setting affect the characters and influence the plot?

4. Identify dialogue between Beneatha and Mama near the end of the scene in which they discuss respect, dignity, and love. Analyze the relationship between characters, and explain how their exchange reveals a theme of the play.

5. Why is owning a home so important to Mama? What makes a home so important to a family? Identify textual evidence to support your answer.

WRITE

LITERARY ANALYSIS: In both "The Old Cabin" and *A Raisin in the Sun*, the historical setting plays an important role in the development of the texts' themes. Identify the historical setting of each text. Then, analyze how the setting of each text impacts each text's themes. Support your response with evidence from the text and your own analysis.

Letter from Chief John Ross

ARGUMENTATIVE TEXT
John Ross
1835

Introduction

John Ross (1790–1866) was a man of mixed racial identity who became Principal Chief of the Cherokee Nation, whose territory was in present-day Georgia. He wrote this letter to the United States Senate and the House of Representatives on September 28, 1836. At that time, the president was Andrew Jackson, who was committed to moving Native Americans west of the Mississippi River so that whites could have their land. The Georgia government had harassed the Cherokees in many ways—seizing their land, suppressing their newspapers, dissolving their government, and even jailing white missionaries who were sympathetic to them. Ross's letter is in response to the Treaty of New Echota, made between the U.S. government and a small group of Cherokee. This treaty gave the Cherokee five million dollars in exchange for their moving to Northeast Oklahoma. Eventually they were forced to move; the cruel march west killed 4,000 and became known as the Trail of Tears.

"We are deprived of membership in the human family!"

1   It is well known that for a number of years past we have been harassed by a series of vexations, which it is deemed unnecessary to recite in detail, but the evidence of which our delegation will be prepared to furnish. With a view to bringing our troubles to a close, a delegation was appointed on the 23rd of October, 1835, by the General Council of the nation,[1] clothed with full powers to enter into arrangements with the Government of the United States, for the final adjustment of all our existing difficulties. The delegation failing to **effect** an arrangement with the United States commissioner, then in the nation, proceeded, agreeably to their instructions in that case, to Washington City, for the purpose of negotiating a treaty with the authorities of the United States.

Chief John Ross

2   After the departure of the Delegation, a contract was made by the Rev. John F. Schermerhorn, and certain individual Cherokees, purporting to be a "treaty, concluded at New Echota, in the State of Georgia, on the 29th day of December, 1835, by General William Carroll and John F. Schermerhorn, commissioners on the part of the United States, and the chiefs, headmen, and people of the Cherokee tribes of Indians." A spurious Delegation, in violation of a special injunction of the general council of the nation, proceeded to Washington City with this pretended treaty, and by false and fraudulent representations **supplanted** in the favor of the Government the legal and accredited Delegation of the Cherokee people,[2] and obtained for this instrument, after making important alterations in its provisions, the recognition of the United States Government. And now it is presented to us as a treaty, ratified by the Senate, and approved by the President [Andrew Jackson], and

---

1. **General Council of the nation** a governing body of the Cherokee
2. **Delegation of the Cherokee people** a selection of people tasked with defending the rights of the Cherokee people against the US Supreme Court

---

Skill: Technical Language

From context, I think "ratify" and "sanction" both relate to giving formal consent to a treaty since they are synonyms for "approve" used in the same sentence. By using these legal terms, Ross makes his tone more authoritative.

Letter from Chief John Ross

NOTES

> our acquiescence in its requirements demanded, under the sanction of the displeasure of the United States, and the threat of **summary** compulsion, in case of refusal. It comes to us, not through our legitimate authorities, the known and usual medium of communication between the Government of the United States and our nation, but through the agency of a complication of powers, civil and military.

Skill: Reasons and Evidence

Ross supports his claim with persuasive concrete examples of what the treaty does to his people. Powerful language and clear examples strengthen his argument.

3   By the stipulations of this instrument, we are despoiled of our private possessions, the indefeasible property of individuals. We are stripped of every attribute of freedom and eligibility for legal self-defence. Our property may be plundered before our eyes; violence may be committed on our persons; even our lives may be taken away, and there is none to regard our complaints. We are denationalized; we are disfranchised. We are deprived of membership in the human family! We have neither land nor home, nor resting place that can be called our own. And this is effected by the provisions of a **compact** which assumes the venerated, the sacred appellation of treaty.

4   We are overwhelmed! Our hearts are sickened, our utterance is paralyzed, when we reflect on the condition in which we are placed, by the audacious practices of unprincipled men, who have managed their stratagems with so much dexterity as to impose on the Government of the United States, in the face of our earnest, solemn, and reiterated protestations.

5   The instrument in question is not the act of our Nation; we are not parties to its covenants; it has not received the sanction of our people. The makers of it sustain no office nor appointment in our Nation, under the designation of Chiefs, Head men, or any other title, by which they hold, or could acquire, authority to assume the reins of Government, and to make bargain and sale of our rights, our possessions, and our common country. And we are constrained solemnly to declare, that we cannot but contemplate the enforcement of the stipulations of this instrument on us, against our consent, as an act of injustice and oppression, which, we are well persuaded, can never knowingly be countenanced by the Government and people of the United States; nor can we believe it to be the design of these honorable and high minded individuals, who stand at the head of the Govt., to **bind** a whole Nation, by the acts of a few unauthorized individuals. And, therefore, we, the parties to be affected by the result, appeal with confidence to the justice, the magnanimity, the compassion, of your honorable bodies, against the enforcement, on us, of the provisions of a compact, in the formation of which we have had no agency.

Skill: Language, Style, and Audience

Ross uses certain words such as "high-minded" to flatter his audience. Then he appeals to the government's sense of "justice" and "compassion." He is trying to make a distinction between his audience and the men who drafted the treaty.

The Papers of Chief John Ross, vol 1, 1807–1839, Norman OK
Gary E. Moulton, ed.
University of Oklahoma Press, 1985

First Read

Read "Letter from Chief John Ross." After you read, complete the Think Questions below.

THINK QUESTIONS

1. What makes this letter especially persuasive? Use evidence from the text about the content and the author's style to support your answer.

2. Describe the overall tone of the letter, meaning the writer's attitude toward the subject or audience. Use evidence from the text to explain your views.

3. Judging only from the letter, what is your evaluation of Ross as a leader? Support your opinion with evidence from the text.

4. Read the following dictionary entry:

   compact
   compact\com•pact\

   noun

   1. an agreement
   2. a small makeup case

   adjective

   3. not taking much space
   4. not wordy

   Decide which definition best matches **compact** as it is used in "Letter from Chief John Ross." Write that definition of *compact* here, and indicate which clues found in the text helped you determine the meaning.

5. What is the meaning of the word **summary** as it is used in the text? Write your best definition of the word *summary* here, along with a brief explanation of how you arrived at its meaning.

Letter from Chief John Ross

Skill: Language, Style, And Audience

Use the Checklist to analyze Language, Style, and Audience in "Letter from Chief John Ross." Refer to the sample student annotations about Language, Style, and Audience in the text.

CHECKLIST FOR LANGUAGE, STYLE, AND AUDIENCE

In order to determine an author's style and possible intended audience, do the following:

- ✓ identify instances where the author uses key terms throughout the course of a text
- ✓ examine surrounding words and phrases to determine the context, connotation, style, and tone of the term
- ✓ analyze how the author's treatment of the key term affects the reader's understanding of the text
- ✓ note the audience—both intended and unintended—and possible reactions to the author's word choice, style, and treatment of key terms

To analyze how an author's treatment of language and key terms affect the reader's understanding of the text, consider the following questions:

- ✓ How do the author's word choices enhance or change what is being described?
- ✓ How do the author's word choices affect the reader's understanding of key terms and ideas in the text?
- ✓ How do choices about language affect the author's style and audience?
- ✓ How often does the author use this term or terms?

Skill: Language, Style, And Audience

Reread paragraphs 3–4 of "Letter from Chief John Ross." Then, using the Checklist on the previous page, answer the multiple-choice questions below.

YOUR TURN

1. What does Ross's choice of the words *denationalized* and *disfranchised* help the reader conclude?

   - A. that the treaty will destroy their land and their homes and that they will have nowhere to sleep
   - B. that the treaty will destroy their nation by denying them their land, freedom, and humanity
   - C. that the treaty is unfair and unjust and is going to make them sick and paralyzed
   - D. that the treaty will take away their private possessions and separate their families

2. What additional piece of textual evidence from this passage supports the correct conclusion in question 1?

   - A. "Our property may be plundered before our eyes; violence may be committed on our persons; . . ."
   - B. "And this is effected by the provisions of a compact which assumes the venerated, the sacred appellation of treaty."
   - C. "Our hearts are sickened, our utterance is paralyzed, when we reflect on the condition in which we are placed . . ."
   - D. "We are deprived of membership in the human family!"

3. What do the intentional word choices in the following statement imply about the author's tone toward those that are imposing this treaty?

"Our hearts are sickened, our utterance is paralyzed, when we reflect on the condition in which we are placed, by the audacious practices of unprincipled men."

- A. The words *sickened, audacious,* and *unprincipled* imply a tone of exhaustion and surrender.
- B. The words *sickened, audacious,* and *unprincipled* imply a tone of discouragement and sadness.
- C. The words *sickened, audacious,* and *unprincipled* imply a tone of astonishment and mistrust.
- D. The words *sickened, audacious,* and *unprincipled* imply a tone of sickness and weakness.

Skill: Technical Language

Use the Checklist to analyze Technical Language in "Letter from Chief John Ross." Refer to the sample student annotations about Technical Language in the text.

CHECKLIST FOR TECHNICAL LANGUAGE

In order to determine the meaning of words and phrases as they are used in a text, including technical meanings, note the following:

- ✓ the subject of the text
- ✓ any unfamiliar words that you think might be technical terms
- ✓ words that have multiple meanings that change when used with a specific subject
- ✓ the possible contextual meaning of a word, or the definition from a dictionary

To determine the meaning of words and phrases as they are used in a text, including technical meanings, consider the following questions:

- ✓ What is the subject of the informational text?
- ✓ How does the use of technical language help establish the author as an authority on a subject?
- ✓ Are there any technical words that have an impact on the meaning and tone of the text?
- ✓ Does the author use the same term several times, refining its meaning and adding layers to it over the course of the text?

Letter from Chief John Ross

Skill: Technical Language

Reread paragraph 5 of "Letter from Chief John Ross." Then, using the Checklist on the previous page, answer the multiple-choice questions below.

YOUR TURN

1. What are the multiple meanings of the word *parties* as the word is used in this passage?

   - A. a group of people going to a party and a group of people affected by something bad
   - B. a group of people taking a side and a group of people with a common goal
   - C. a group of people who belong to a political party and a group of people who like each other
   - D. a group of people taking part in something and a group of people in the same political party

2. What is the meaning of the word *agency* in the context of this letter? Consider a meaning for this word that you may know, and then use that knowledge to determine its meaning in the context of this text.

   - A. the duty or function of an agent
   - B. the capacity of individuals to act independently and make their own choices
   - C. an organization, company or government office that provides a service for another
   - D. a large vehicle

Skill: Reasons and Evidence

Use the Checklist to analyze Reasons and Evidence in "Letter from Chief John Ross." Refer to the sample student annotations about Reasons and Evidence in the text.

CHECKLIST FOR REASONS AND EVIDENCE

In order to delineate and evaluate the reasoning in seminal U.S. texts, note the following:

- ✓ the writer's position and argument
- ✓ how the writer uses legal or other reasoning to interpret a legal conflict
  - legal reasoning includes the thinking processes and strategies used by lawyers and judges when arguing and deciding legal cases, and is based on constitutional principles, or laws written down in the U.S. Constitution
  - other reasoning includes that based on the accepted general principles of logic
- ✓ the precision of the author's argument or how exactly he or she identifies conflicts, claims, objections, and supporting evidence
- ✓ how compelling the writer's argument is and the elements that give the argument force and power and those that lessen its strength and viability
- ✓ whether the premise is based on legal reasoning and constitutional principles and/or upon moral or ethical principles

To evaluate the reasoning in seminal U.S. texts consider the following questions:

- ✓ What position does the writer take?
- ✓ How does the writer use reasoning and evidence to support his or her position?
- ✓ What gives the argument strength?
- ✓ What weakens its power?

Skill: Reasons and Evidence

Reread paragraph 5 of "Letter from Chief John Ross." Then, using the Checklist on the previous page, answer the multiple-choice questions below.

YOUR TURN

1. What is the main claim that Chief Ross makes in the closing of his letter?

   - A. The treaty is cruel and exemplifies the government's hatred of the Cherokee peoples.
   - B. The U.S. government is unfair and consistently takes advantage of native populations.
   - C. The Cherokee treaty makers were not chiefs and therefore don't have authority to make a treaty.
   - D. The government should not enforce the treaty, as it is invalid.

2. What reasoning does Ross use in this passage to support his main claim?

   - A. The treaty was drafted without his tribe's consent, and therefore it should not be enforced.
   - B. If the U.S. government enforces the treaty, then countless people will be harmed.
   - C. The treaty divides the tribe's property unevenly, and a more fair distribution should be reached.
   - D. The Cherokee people will rebel if the treaty is enforced.

Close Read

Reread "Letter from Chief John Ross." As you reread, complete the Skills Focus questions below. Then use your answers and annotations from the questions to help you complete the Write activity.

SKILLS FOCUS

1. Identify examples in the beginning of Chief John Ross's letter that illustrate how his choice of precise words informs and shapes the perception of his readers. Explain the topic of his letter.

2. The word *treaty* is used throughout the letter. Find the word in the text, and determine its meaning using context clues. Explain how you arrived at this meaning.

3. What evidence does Chief John Ross provide to support the idea that the treaty is not valid? Identify his evidence, and explain how his evidence and reasoning support his claim.

4. Identify evidence that Ross wanted his audience to understand that his people had tried to let the government know what had happened. Explain what the Cherokees did and how this evidence supports Ross's claim.

5. Where do we see evidence that land, nature, and community are sacred to John Ross and his people? Explain why this aspect of their identity makes the atrocities of the U.S. government especially hurtful.

WRITE

RHETORICAL ANALYSIS: Chief John Ross worked to attain rights and respect for his people in the face of oppression by the United States government. In this letter, how does Ross use style, tone, and word choice to achieve his purpose? Evaluate Ross's use of persuasive language as well as reasons and evidence to convince his audience. Support your response with evidence from the text and your own commentary.

Dream House

ARGUMENTATIVE TEXT
Point/Counterpoint
2018

Introduction

For generations, owning a home has been a milestone on the road through adulthood, and a primary benchmark by which we evaluate our success in pursuing the American Dream. But as the economy changes, and a new crop of adults takes control of the culture around family and career, this tradition is being reconsidered and even, in some cases, abandoned entirely. Does this represent a downturn in our priorities, or have we found a new way to prosperity? Both essays present strong opinions about the importance of home ownership in our lives. Which do you find more persuasive?

"Home ownership is a part of our national character..."

Dream Home: Is owning a home essential to the American Dream?

Point: Home Ownership Is the Foundation of the American Dream.

1. Anyone who has played the classic board game the Game of Life or the video game *The Sims* knows that owning a home is the **modus operandi** for many Americans. Before players can advance in either of these popular games, they must first buy or build a home; renting is not even presented as an option. It would seem that the gamemakers agree with the more than 80% of young adults who, according to the National Association of Realtors, believe that home ownership is a good investment. Still, Americans are motivated by more than the chance of a strong return on investment: buying a home, especially a first home, is an emotional milestone that many Americans strive to achieve. Like settlers moving west on the American frontier, contemporary Americans seek the freedom and satisfaction that come from owning a piece of the country we call home. Home ownership is a part of our national character and a key feature of what many see as the American Dream, so that leads many Americans to choose home ownership over renting.

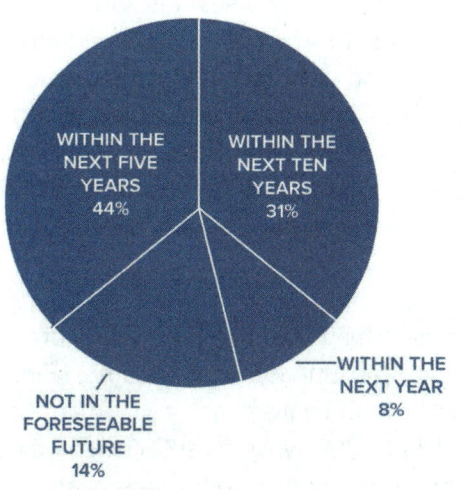

NON-HOMEOWNERS IN 2017 WHO EXPECT TO BUY HOMES SOON AMONG THOSE 18-34

credit: https://news.gallup.com/poll/210008/half-non-homeowners-expect-buy-homes-five-years.aspx

Owning Means Freedom

2   As renters, tenants have to follow specific rules; for example, tenants have to request permission to modify their landlord's property and may not be able to personalize their living space as much as they would like. As homeowners, people can renovate and remodel frequently and extensively, including painting walls, changing fixtures, overhauling the yard, or even knocking down walls to make a space feel like home. By purchasing a home, homeowners can do whatever they want to their property; for this reason, many people choose to buy homes instead of continuing to rent.

3   Furthermore, homeowners can set their own rules about how and when they want to use their living areas, which includes decisions about noise levels, owning pets, and having extended-stay guests. Many landlords prohibit cats, dogs, and other pets, and they may have restrictive noise policies with stiff penalties. Many people find these kinds of rules annoying; people don't like unnecessary rules, such as rules that prevent people from keeping their garbage cans in front of their property. Homeowners are free to decide the behaviors and occupants of their own homes without worrying about breaking arbitrary policies set to appease a landlord's whims.

Owning Means Stability

4   Another drawback to renting is that renters often move from place to place. They may have to move because of annual increases in the cost of rent or because their landlords are selling the property. Once homeowners have purchased a home, their mortgage payment remains static and, provided they pay the mortgage on time every month, no one can evict them and sell the property to someone else. Unlike renters who have to accept new rental terms and sign a new lease every year, homeowners can rest easy knowing that their lives will remain stable for many years.

5   In addition to the stability of having regular mortgage payments, some claim that having a mortgage is actually a form of forced savings, which offers an additional layer of financial stability. As borrowers make their mortgage payments, they pay part of the interest and part of the borrowed amount, so each payment builds the buyer's home equity. Homeowners can borrow against that equity later to make home improvements, or they can use the equity to make a down payment on a new house. For people who have trouble saving separately, paying into a mortgage may help them save for the future.

6   Due to this forced savings, homeowners may also be financially more sound than renters. Per the Federal Reserve's Survey of Consumer Finances, homeowners have a higher net worth than renters; as of 2013, an average homeowner's net worth was around $195,000 while a renter's net worth was $5,400. The same discrepancies can apply to what homeowners and renters

pay for their respective living spaces. In 2018, the National Low Income Housing Coalition found that the Fair Market Rent for a two-bedroom is $1,149 a month. Depending on the house and the down payment, homeowners might be able to get more space for a lower monthly rate—a rate that does not change unless the house is refinanced. Rates for renters, on the other hand, can always go up depending on the landlord's discretion.

Owning Means Sense of Well-Being

7   Home ownership comes with many benefits, but one of the most satisfying is the sense of well-being that comes with owning a property. Above all, a property you own is a place where you can **cultivate** a life, make memories, and plan for a secure future. All those things bring about a sense of satisfaction that cannot be achieved by renting, especially since the money spent on rent is gone as soon as it is sent while the money you invest in a home is there to stay. Nothing can replace that feeling of security and happiness of investing in your own future.

8   Although home ownerships may come with unexpected surprises, owning your own property will always give you more freedom, greater stability, and ultimately the best sense of well-being that money can buy.

"[An] American Dream that hinges on home ownership may soon be a relic of a long-forgotten past."

Counterpoint: Renting Is the New American Dream.

9. Although some people dream of owning a big house in the suburbs with a white picket fence where they can raise their 2.5 kids and watch their golden retriever frolic in the yard, that is not everyone's idea of the American Dream. For many people, exploration is their **raison d'être**, so it is more important, more fulfilling, and more practical to rent than to own property. In fact, the version of the American Dream that hinges on home ownership may soon be a relic of a long-forgotten past; according to the Pew Research Center, more Americans are renting now than they have at any time in the last 50 years.

Renting Means Less Expense

10. In order to buy a home, most buyers are required to pull together a down payment of about 20% of the house's purchase price. For a home that costs even $100,000, which is a quarter of the national average price for a new home, that means a buyer would have to save at least $20,000. Most young adults do not have that kind of cash on hand, especially considering the fact that young adults have a high rate of student loan debt—a collective figure of around $1.5 trillion as of early 2018.

11. Even if potential buyers are able to save $20,000, they are unlikely to find a home within their price range. As of 2017, the number of homes priced below $100,000 dropped by 13% nationally, meaning that lower-priced houses are not as abundant and therefore will have more demand. At the same time, the number of homes priced between $500,000 and $750,000 increased by 12%, so more expensive homes are more widely available. For the low end of these higher priced houses, buyers would need to save a minimum of $100,000 for a 20% down payment, or roughly the out-of-state tuition cost of four years at a public four-year college. For a recent graduate, this kind of down payment is probably too hefty.

12. Down payment aside, homeowners face other upfront expenses when purchasing a home, and these expenses, called closing costs, can include:
    - Application fees
    - Appraisal fees

- Attorney fees
- Property taxes
- Mortgage insurance
- Home inspection
- First year homeowner's insurance premium
- Title search
- Title insurance
- Prepaid interest
- Origination fees
- Recording fees
- Survey fees

13 Closing costs often add up to about 5% of the cost of the house, which pushes the price of owning up even higher.

Renting Means Others Repair

14 In a house or in other privately owned properties, the owner is responsible for any and all repairs that need to be made. Because the owner makes repairs, that means that the owner is responsible for the property. For renters, any repairs needed on a property (unless it is the tenant's fault) are **gratis**; the landlord has to pay. That means that renters do not need to worry about the additional expenses associated with broken appliances, busted pipes, and damage caused by natural disasters.

15 Although tenants face strict policies against changing the property they're renting, that limitation actually becomes an asset in the long run. Instead of spending money on surface-level renovations, such as painting or planting flowers, renters can save their money for other life-enhancing expenses, such as travel or entertainment.

Renting Means Mobility

16 In order to make back the money they put into a property, homeowners often need to stay in a property for at least five years. On the other hand, renters have to stay in the same place only as long as the terms of their lease require. At the end of each lease term, renters can choose to either renew or move on to their next adventure. This mobility is particularly useful when a job opportunity opens up in a new city or country. Homeowners may have trouble selling their property, but renters can just pick up and leave.

17 Additionally, if a property comes with nasty surprises like discourteous neighbors or challenges due to local wildlife, homeowners have to learn to live with disappointment or go through the hassle of selling a problematic

property. Renters, on the other hand, only have to wait until the end of a lease to escape hidden apartment issues or annoying neighbors.

Renting Means Freedom

18 Embedded in all the reasons above is the overarching idea that renting means more freedom; by relieving themselves of the worries that come with home ownership, renters can instead focus on what they really want to get out of life: new experiences. It is clear that Americans like to have a **plethora** of choices; that's why megastores and large online retailers are so popular. They may want to pursue a career in a new field, go back to school, or travel around the world for extended periods of time; although these options may still be possible if you own a home, the costs and responsibilities associated with owning a property can complicate these plans.

19 If you imagine your life will include more than mowing grass and fixing your leaky roof, then renting is the right choice for you. As Americans, we all want the freedom to live the way we choose and to pursue our passions; the best way to achieve that is to ditch the mortgage and sign a lease.

WRITE

ARGUMENTATIVE: The authors of the Point and Counterpoint essays make opposing arguments about the importance of owning a home. Which of the two essays do you find more convincing and why? Support your answer with relevant evidence from the text. You may choose to include evidence from graphic features.

The Fall of the House of Usher

FICTION
Edgar Allan Poe
1839

Introduction

Edgar Allan Poe (1809–1849), aside from inventing the detective story, was also one of the early innovators of Gothic horror. "The Fall of the House of Usher" is one of Poe's most famous short stories, containing many familiar elements readers will encounter throughout his work: the innocent narrator called on for help; the family curse; the creepy, disintegrating old house; and a mysterious body of water (the *tarn*) that contains a possible source of evil. These now-familiar *tropes*, as they are called, continue to appear in horror novels, stories, and films to the present day. It was all here, first, brought to life by Poe's no-holds-barred language and his commitment to the lurid scare.

"... oh, pity me, miserable wretch that I am!—I dared not—I dared not speak!"

Son cœur est un luth suspendu;
*Sitôt qu'on le touche il résonne.**

(*His/her heart is a poised lute;*
As soon as it is touched, it resounds)

De Béranger.

Edgar Allan Poe

1   During the whole of a dull, dark, and soundless day in the autumn of the year, when the clouds hung oppressively low in the heavens, I had been passing alone, on horseback, through a singularly dreary tract of country, and at length found myself, as the shades of the evening drew on, within view of the melancholy House of Usher. I know not how it was—but, with the first glimpse of the building, a sense of **insufferable** gloom pervaded my spirit. I say insufferable; for the feeling was unrelieved by any of that half-pleasurable, because poetic, sentiment, with which the mind usually receives even the sternest natural images of the desolate or terrible. I looked upon the scene before me—upon the mere house, and the simple landscape features of the domain—upon the bleak walls—upon the vacant eye-like windows—upon a few rank sedges—and upon a few white trunks of decayed trees—with an utter depression of soul which I can compare to no earthly sensation more properly than to the after-dream of the reveller upon opium—the bitter lapse into every-day life—the hideous dropping off of the veil. There was an iciness, a sinking, a sickening of the heart—an unredeemed dreariness of thought which no goading of the imagination could torture into aught of the sublime. What was it—I paused to think—what was it that so unnerved me in the contemplation of the House of Usher? It was a mystery all insoluble; nor could I grapple with the shadowy fancies that crowded upon me as I pondered. I was forced to fall back upon the unsatisfactory conclusion, that while, beyond doubt, there *are* combinations of very simple natural objects which have the power of thus affecting us, still the analysis of this power lies among considerations beyond

our depth. It was possible, I reflected, that a mere different arrangement of the particulars of the scene, of the details of the picture, would be sufficient to modify, or perhaps to annihilate its capacity for sorrowful impression; and, acting upon this idea, I reined my horse to the precipitous brink of a black and lurid tarn that lay in unruffled lustre by the dwelling, and gazed down—but with a shudder even more thrilling than before—upon the remodelled and inverted images of the gray sedge, and the ghastly tree-stems, and the vacant and eye-like windows.

2   Nevertheless, in this mansion of gloom I now proposed to myself a sojourn of some weeks. Its proprietor, Roderick Usher, had been one of my boon companions in boyhood; but many years had elapsed since our last meeting. A letter, however, had lately reached me in a distant part of the country—a letter from him—which, in its wildly importunate nature, had admitted of no other than a personal reply. The MS. gave evidence of nervous agitation. The writer spoke of acute bodily illness—of a mental disorder which oppressed him—and of an earnest desire to see me, as his best and indeed his only personal friend, with a view of attempting, by the cheerfulness of my society, some alleviation of his **malady**. It was the manner in which all this, and much more, was said—it was the apparent *heart* that went with his request—which allowed me no room for hesitation; and I accordingly obeyed forthwith what I still considered a very singular summons.

3   Although, as boys, we had been even intimate associates, yet I really knew little of my friend. His reserve had been always excessive and habitual. I was aware, however, that his very ancient family had been noted, time out of mind, for a peculiar sensibility of temperament, displaying itself, through long ages, in many works of exalted art, and manifested, of late, in repeated deeds of **munificent** yet unobtrusive charity, as well as in a passionate devotion to the intricacies, perhaps even more than to the orthodox and easily recognizable beauties, of musical science. I had learned, too, the very remarkable fact, that the stem of the Usher race, all time-honored as it was, had put forth, at no period, any enduring branch; in other words, that the entire family lay in the direct line of descent, and had always, with very trifling and very temporary variation, so lain. It was this deficiency, I considered, while running over in thought the perfect keeping of the character of the premises with the accredited character of the people, and while speculating upon the possible influence which the one, in the long lapse of centuries, might have exercised upon the other—it was this deficiency, perhaps, of collateral issue, and the consequent undeviating transmission, from sire to son, of the patrimony with the name, which had, at length, so identified the two as to merge the original title of the estate in the quaint and equivocal appellation of the "House of Usher"—an appellation which seemed to include, in the minds of the peasantry who used it, both the family and the family mansion.

4 I have said that the sole effect of my somewhat childish experiment—that of looking down within the tarn—had been to deepen the first singular impression. There can be no doubt that the consciousness of the rapid increase of my superstition—for why should I not so term it?—served mainly to accelerate the increase itself. Such, I have long known, is the paradoxical law of all sentiments having terror as a basis. And it might have been for this reason only, that, when I again uplifted my eyes to the house itself, from its image in the pool, there grew in my mind a strange fancy—a fancy so ridiculous, indeed, that I but mention it to show the vivid force of the sensations which oppressed me. I had so worked upon my imagination as really to believe that about the whole mansion and domain there hung an atmosphere peculiar to themselves and their immediate vicinity—an atmosphere which had no affinity with the air of heaven, but which had reeked up from the decayed trees, and the gray wall, and the silent tarn—a pestilent and mystic vapor, dull, sluggish, faintly discernible, and leaden-hued.

5 Shaking off from my spirit what *must* have been a dream, I scanned more narrowly the real aspect of the building. Its principal feature seemed to be that of an excessive antiquity. The discoloration of ages had been great. Minute fungi overspread the whole exterior, hanging in a fine tangled web-work from the eaves. Yet all this was apart from any extraordinary dilapidation. No portion of the masonry had fallen; and there appeared to be a wild inconsistency between its still perfect adaptation of parts, and the crumbling condition of the individual stones. In this there was much that reminded me of the specious totality of old wood-work which has rotted for long years in some neglected vault, with no disturbance from the breath of the external air. Beyond this indication of extensive decay, however, the fabric gave little token of instability. Perhaps the eye of a scrutinizing observer might have discovered a barely perceptible fissure, which, extending from the roof of the building in front, made its way down the wall in a zigzag direction, until it became lost in the sullen waters of the tarn.

6 Noticing these things, I rode over a short causeway to the house. A servant in waiting took my horse, and I entered the Gothic archway of the hall. A valet, of **stealthy** step, thence conducted me, in silence, through many dark and intricate passages in my progress to the *studio* of his master. Much that I encountered on the way contributed, I know not how, to heighten the vague sentiments of which I have already spoken. While the objects around me—while the carvings of the ceilings, the sombre tapestries of the walls, the ebon blackness of the floors, and the phantasmagoric armorial trophies which rattled as I strode, were but matters to which, or to such as which, I had been accustomed from my infancy—while I hesitated not to acknowledge how familiar was all this—I still wondered to find how unfamiliar were the fancies which ordinary images were stirring up. On one of the staircases, I met the physician of the family. His

countenance, I thought, wore a mingled expression of low cunning and perplexity. He accosted me with **trepidation** and passed on. The valet now threw open a door and ushered me into the presence of his master.

7   The room in which I found myself was very large and lofty. The windows were long, narrow, and pointed, and at so vast a distance from the black oaken floor as to be altogether inaccessible from within. Feeble gleams of encrimsoned light made their way through the trellised panes, and served to render sufficiently distinct the more prominent objects around; the eye, however, struggled in vain to reach the remoter angles of the chamber, or the recesses of the vaulted and fretted ceiling. Dark draperies hung upon the walls. The general furniture was profuse, comfortless, antique, and tattered. Many books and musical instruments lay scattered about, but failed to give any vitality to the scene. I felt that I breathed an atmosphere of sorrow. An air of stern, deep, and irredeemable gloom hung over and pervaded all.

8   Upon my entrance, Usher rose from a sofa on which he had been lying at full length, and greeted me with a vivacious warmth which had much in it, I at first thought, of an overdone cordiality—of the constrained effort of the *ennuyé* man of the world. A glance, however, at his countenance convinced me of his perfect sincerity. We sat down; and for some moments, while he spoke not, I gazed upon him with a feeling half of pity, half of awe. Surely, man had never before so terribly altered, in so brief a period, as had Roderick Usher! It was with difficulty that I could bring myself to admit the identity of the wan being before me with the companion of my early boyhood. Yet the character of his face had been at all times remarkable. A cadaverousness of complexion; an eye large, liquid, and luminous beyond comparison; lips somewhat thin and very pallid, but of a surpassingly beautiful curve; a nose of a delicate Hebrew model, but with a breadth of nostril unusual in similar formations; a finely moulded chin, speaking, in its want of prominence, of a want of moral energy; hair of a more than web-like softness and tenuity;—these features, with an inordinate expansion above the regions of the temple, made up altogether a countenance not easily to be forgotten. And now in the mere exaggeration of the prevailing character of these features, and of the expression they were wont to convey, lay so much of change that I doubted to whom I spoke. The now ghastly pallor of the skin, and the now miraculous lustre of the eye, above all things startled and even awed me. The silken hair, too, had been suffered to grow all unheeded, and as, in its wild gossamer texture, it floated rather than fell about the face, I could not, even with effort, connect its Arabesque expression with any idea of simple humanity.

9   In the manner of my friend I was at once struck with an incoherence—an inconsistency; and I soon found this to arise from a series of feeble and futile struggles to overcome an habitual trepidancy—an excessive nervous

agitation. For something of this nature I had indeed been prepared, no less by his letter, than by reminiscences of certain boyish traits, and by conclusions deduced from his peculiar physical conformation and temperament. His action was alternately vivacious and sullen. His voice varied rapidly from a tremulous indecision (when the animal spirits seemed utterly in abeyance) to that species of energetic concision—that abrupt, weighty, unhurried, and hollow-sounding enunciation—that leaden, self-balanced and perfectly modulated guttural utterance, which may be observed in the lost drunkard, or the irreclaimable eater of opium, during the periods of his most intense excitement.

10 It was thus that he spoke of the object of my visit, of his earnest desire to see me, and of the solace he expected me to afford him. He entered, at some length, into what he conceived to be the nature of his malady. It was, he said, a constitutional and a family evil, and one for which he despaired to find a remedy—a mere nervous affection, he immediately added, which would undoubtedly soon pass off. It displayed itself in a host of unnatural sensations. Some of these, as he detailed them, interested and bewildered me; although, perhaps, the terms and the general manner of the narration had their weight. He suffered much from a morbid acuteness of the senses; the most insipid food was alone endurable; he could wear only garments of certain texture; the odors of all flowers were oppressive; his eyes were tortured by even a faint light; and there were but peculiar sounds, and these from stringed instruments, which did not inspire him with horror.

11 To an anomalous species of terror I found him a bounden slave. "I shall perish," said he, "I *must* perish in this deplorable folly. Thus, thus, and not otherwise, shall I be lost. I dread the events of the future, not in themselves, but in their results. I shudder at the thought of any, even the most trivial, incident, which may operate upon this intolerable agitation of soul. I have, indeed, no abhorrence of danger, except in its absolute effect—in terror. In this unnerved, in this pitiable, condition I feel that the period will sooner or later arrive when I must abandon life and reason together, in some struggle with the grim phantasm, FEAR."

12 I learned, moreover, at intervals, and through broken and equivocal hints, another singular feature of his mental condition. He was enchained by certain superstitious impressions in regard to the dwelling which he tenanted, and whence, for many years, he had never ventured forth—in regard to an influence whose supposititious force was conveyed in terms too shadowy here to be re-stated—an influence which some peculiarities in the mere form and substance of his family mansion had, by dint of long sufferance, he said, obtained over his spirit—an effect which the *physique* of the gray walls and

turrets, and of the dim tarn into which they all looked down, had, at length, brought about upon the *morale* of his existence.

13 He admitted, however, although with hesitation, that much of the peculiar gloom which thus afflicted him could be traced to a more natural and far more palpable origin—to the severe and long-continued illness—indeed to the evidently approaching dissolution—of a tenderly beloved sister, his sole companion for long years, his last and only relative on earth. "Her decease," he said, with a bitterness which I can never forget, "would leave him (him the hopeless and the frail) the last of the ancient race of the Ushers." While he spoke, the lady Madeline (for so was she called) passed slowly through a remote portion of the apartment, and, without having noticed my presence, disappeared. I regarded her with an utter astonishment not unmingled with dread; and yet I found it impossible to account for such feelings. A sensation of stupor oppressed me as my eyes followed her retreating steps. When a door, at length, closed upon her, my glance sought instinctively and eagerly the countenance of the brother; but he had buried his face in his hands, and I could only perceive that a far more than ordinary wanness had overspread the emaciated fingers through which trickled many passionate tears.

14 The disease of the lady Madeline had long baffled the skill of her physicians. A settled apathy, a gradual wasting away of the person, and frequent although transient affections of a partially cataleptical character were the unusual diagnosis. Hitherto she had steadily borne up against the pressure of her malady, and had not betaken herself finally to bed; but on the closing in of the evening of my arrival at the house, she succumbed (as her brother told me at night with inexpressible agitation) to the prostrating power of the destroyer; and I learned that the glimpse I had obtained of her person would thus probably be the last I should obtain—that the lady, at least while living, would be seen by me no more.

15 For several days ensuing, her name was unmentioned by either Usher or myself; and during this period I was busied in earnest endeavors to alleviate the melancholy of my friend. We painted and read together, or I listened, as if in a dream, to the wild improvisations of his speaking guitar. And thus, as a closer and still closer intimacy admitted me more unreservedly into the recesses of his spirit, the more bitterly did I perceive the futility of all attempt at cheering a mind from which darkness, as if an inherent positive quality, poured forth upon all objects of the moral and physical universe in one unceasing radiation of gloom.

16 I shall ever bear about me a memory of the many solemn hours I thus spent alone with the master of the House of Usher. Yet I should fail in any attempt to convey an idea of the exact character of the studies, or of the occupations, in

which he involved me, or led me the way. An excited and highly distempered ideality threw a sulphureous lustre over all. His long improvised dirges will ring forever in my ears. Among other things, I hold painfully in mind a certain singular perversion and amplification of the wild air of the last waltz of Von Weber.[1] From the paintings over which his elaborate fancy brooded, and which grew, touch by touch, into vagueness at which I shuddered the more thrillingly, because I shuddered knowing not why—from these paintings (vivid as their images now are before me) I would in vain endeavor to deduce more than a small portion which should lie within the compass of merely written words. By the utter simplicity, by the nakedness of his designs, he arrested and overawed attention. If ever mortal painted an idea, that mortal was Roderick Usher. For me at least, in the circumstances then surrounding me, there arose out of the pure abstractions which the hypochondriac contrived to throw upon his canvas, an intensity of intolerable awe, no shadow of which felt I ever yet in the contemplation of the certainly glowing yet too concrete reveries of Fuseli.[2]

17   One of the phantasmagoric conceptions of my friend, partaking not so rigidly of the spirit of abstraction, may be shadowed forth, although feebly, in words. A small picture presented the interior of an immensely long and rectangular vault or tunnel, with low walls, smooth, white, and without interruption or device. Certain accessory points of the design served well to convey the idea that this excavation lay at an exceeding depth below the surface of the earth. No outlet was observed in any portion of its vast extent, and no torch or other artificial source of light was discernible; yet a flood of intense rays rolled throughout, and bathed the whole in a ghastly and inappropriate splendor.

18   I have just spoken of that morbid condition of the auditory nerve which rendered all music intolerable to the sufferer, with the exception of certain effects of stringed instruments. It was, perhaps, the narrow limits to which he thus confined himself upon the guitar which gave birth, in great measure, to the fantastic character of the performances. But the fervid *facility* of his *impromptus* could not be so accounted for. They must have been, and were, in the notes, as well as in the words of his wild fantasias (for he not unfrequently accompanied himself with rhymed verbal improvisations), the result of that intense mental collectedness and concentration to which I have previously alluded as observable only in particular moments of the highest artificial excitement. The words of one of these rhapsodies I have easily remembered. I was, perhaps, the more forcibly impressed with it as he gave it, because, in the under or mystic current of its meaning, I fancied that I perceived, and for the first time, a full consciousness on the part of Usher of the tottering of his

---

1. **the last waltz of Von Weber** a famous piece of classical music
2. **Fuseli** a Swiss painter working in the early 19th century, many of whose paintings dealt with supernatural or mythological subject matter

lofty reason upon her throne. The verses, which were entitled "The Haunted Palace," ran very nearly, if not accurately, thus:

I.

In the greenest of our valleys,
    By good angels tenanted,
Once a fair and stately palace—
Radiant palace—reared its head.
In the monarch Thought's dominion—
    It stood there!
Never seraph spread a pinion
    Over fabric half so fair.

II.

Banners yellow, glorious, golden,
    On its roof did float and flow;
(This—all this—was in the olden
    Time long ago);
And every gentle air that dallied,
    In that sweet day,
Along the ramparts plumed and pallid,
    A winged odor went away.

III.

Wanderers in that happy valley
    Through two luminous windows saw
Spirits moving musically
    To a lute's well-tunèd law;
Round about a throne, where sitting
    (Porphyrogene![3])
In state his glory well befitting,
    The ruler of the realm was seen.

IV.

And all with pearl and ruby glowing
    Was the fair palace door,
Through which came flowing, flowing, flowing
    And sparkling evermore,
A troop of Echoes[4] whose sweet duty
    Was but to sing,
In voices of surpassing beauty,
    The wit and wisdom of their king.

---

3. **Porphyrogene** literally "born into purple," purple in this context representing royalty or nobility
4. **Echoes** in Greek mythology, a cave nymph who was cursed by Hera, Zeus's wife, to repeat other people's previous words

V.

23   But evil things, in robes of sorrow,
          Assailed the monarch's high estate;
     (Ah, let us mourn, for never morrow
          Shall dawn upon him, desolate!)
     And, round about his home, the glory
          That blushed and bloomed
     Is but a dim-remembered story
          Of the old time entombed.

VI.

24   And travellers now within that valley,
          Through the red-litten windows see
     Vast forms that move fantastically
          To a discordant melody;
     While, like a rapid ghastly river,
          Through the pale door,
     A hideous throng rush out forever,
          And laugh—but smile no more.

25   I well remember that suggestions arising from this ballad, led us into a train of thought wherein there became manifest an opinion of Usher's which I mention not so much on account of its novelty (for other men have thought thus), as on account of the pertinacity with which he maintained it. This opinion, in its general form, was that of the sentience of all vegetable things. But, in his disordered fancy, the idea had assumed a more daring character, and trespassed, under certain conditions, upon the kingdom of inorganization. I lack words to express the full extent, or the earnest *abandon* of his persuasion. The belief, however, was connected (as I have previously hinted) with the gray stones of the home of his forefathers. The conditions of the sentience had been here, he imagined, fulfilled in the method of collocation of these stones—in the order of their arrangement, as well as in that of the many *fungi* which overspread them, and of the decayed trees which stood around—above all, in the long undisturbed endurance of this arrangement, and in its reduplication in the still waters of the tarn. Its evidence—the evidence of the sentience—was to be seen, he said, (and I here started as he spoke), in the gradual yet certain condensation of an atmosphere of their own about the waters and the walls. The result was discoverable, he added, in that silent yet importunate and terrible influence which for centuries had moulded the destinies of his family, and which made *him* what I now saw him—what he was. Such opinions need no comment, and I will make none.

26   Our books—the books which, for years, had formed no small portion of the mental existence of the invalid—were, as might be supposed, in strict keeping with this character of phantasm. We pored together over such works as the

Ververt et Chartreuse of Gresset; the Belphegor of Machiavelli; the Heaven and Hell of Swedenborg; the Subterranean Voyage of Nicholas Klimm by Holberg; the Chiromancy of Robert Flud, of Jean D'Indaginé, and of De la Chambre; the Journey into the Blue Distance of Tieck; and the City of the Sun of Campanella. One favorite volume was a small octavo edition of the Directorium Inquisitorium, by the Dominican Eymeric de Gironne; and there were passages in Pomponius Mela, about the old African Satyrs and Œgipans, over which Usher would sit dreaming for hours. His chief delight, however, was found in the perusal of an exceedingly rare and curious book in quarto Gothic—the manual of a forgotten church—the Vigiliæ Mortuorum Secundum Chorum Ecclesiæ Maguntinæ.[5]

27 I could not help thinking of the wild ritual of this work, and of its probable influence upon the hypochondriac, when, one evening, having informed me abruptly that the lady Madeline was no more, he stated his intention of preserving her corpse for a fortnight (previously to its final interment), in one of the numerous vaults within the main walls of the building. The worldly reason, however, assigned for this singular proceeding, was one which I did not feel at liberty to dispute. The brother had been led to his resolution (so he told me) by consideration of the unusual character of the malady of the deceased, of certain obtrusive and eager inquiries on the part of her medical men, and of the remote and exposed situation of the burial-ground of the family. I will not deny that when I called to mind the sinister countenance of the person whom I met upon the staircase, on the day of my arrival at the house, I had no desire to oppose what I regarded as at best but a harmless, and by no means an unnatural, precaution.

28 At the request of Usher, I personally aided him in the arrangements for the temporary entombment. The body having been encoffined, we two alone bore it to its rest. The vault in which we placed it (and which had been so long unopened that our torches, half smothered in its oppressive atmosphere, gave us little opportunity for investigation) was small, damp, and entirely without means of admission for light; lying, at great depth, immediately beneath that portion of the building in which was my own sleeping apartment. It had been used, apparently, in remote feudal times, for the worst purposes of a donjon-keep, and, in later days, as a place of deposit for powder, or some other highly combustible substance, as a portion of its floor, and the whole interior of a long archway through which we reached it, were carefully sheathed with copper. The door, of massive iron, had been, also, similarly protected. Its immense weight caused an unusually sharp, grating sound, as it moved upon its hinges.

5. **Vigiliæ Mortuorum Secundum Chorum Ecclesiæ Maguntinæ** the title of a book printed in 1500, translated from Latin: "Vigils for the Dead According to the Use of the Church of Mainz"

The Fall of the House of Usher

29 Having deposited our mournful burden upon tressels within this region of horror, we partially turned aside the yet unscrewed lid of the coffin, and looked upon the face of the tenant. A striking similitude between the brother and sister now first arrested my attention; and Usher, divining, perhaps, my thoughts, murmured out some few words from which I learned that the deceased and himself had been twins, and that sympathies of a scarcely intelligible nature had always existed between them. Our glances, however, rested not long upon the dead—for we could not regard her unawed. The disease which had thus entombed the lady in the maturity of youth, had left, as usual in all maladies of a strictly cataleptical character, the mockery of a faint blush upon the bosom and the face, and that suspiciously lingering smile upon the lip which is so terrible in death. We replaced and screwed down the lid, and, having secured the door of iron, made our way, with toil, into the scarcely less gloomy apartments of the upper portion of the house.

30 And now, some days of bitter grief having elapsed, an observable change came over the features of the mental disorder of my friend. His ordinary manner had vanished. His ordinary occupations were neglected or forgotten. He roamed from chamber to chamber with hurried, unequal, and objectless step. The pallor of his countenance had assumed, if possible, a more ghastly hue—but the luminousness of his eye had utterly gone out. The once occasional huskiness of his tone was heard no more; and a tremulous quaver, as if of extreme terror, habitually characterized his utterance. There were times, indeed, when I thought his unceasingly agitated mind was laboring with some oppressive secret, to divulge which he struggled for the necessary courage. At times, again, I was obliged to resolve all into the mere inexplicable vagaries of madness, for I beheld him gazing upon vacancy for long hours, in an attitude of the profoundest attention, as if listening to some imaginary sound. It was no wonder that his condition terrified—that it infected me. I felt creeping upon me, by slow yet certain degrees, the wild influences of his own fantastic yet impressive superstitions.

31 It was, especially, upon retiring to bed late in the night of the seventh or eighth day after the placing of the lady Madeline within the donjon, that I experienced the full power of such feelings. Sleep came not near my couch—while the hours waned and waned away. I struggled to reason off the nervousness which had dominion over me. I endeavored to believe that much, if not all of what I felt, was due to the bewildering influence of the gloomy furniture of the room—of the dark and tattered draperies, which, tortured into motion by the breath of a rising tempest, swayed fitfully to and fro upon the walls, and rustled uneasily about the decorations of the bed. But my efforts were fruitless. An irrepressible tremor gradually pervaded my frame; and, at length, there sat upon my very heart an incubus of utterly causeless alarm. Shaking this off with a gasp and a struggle, I uplifted myself upon the pillows, and, peering earnestly within the intense darkness of the

chamber, hearkened—I know not why, except that an instinctive spirit prompted me—to certain low and indefinite sounds which came, through the pauses of the storm, at long intervals, I knew not whence. Overpowered by an intense sentiment of horror, unaccountable yet unendurable, I threw on my clothes with haste (for I felt that I should sleep no more during the night), and endeavored to arouse myself from the pitiable condition into which I had fallen, by pacing rapidly to and fro through the apartment.

32   I had taken but few turns in this manner, when a light step on an adjoining staircase arrested my attention. I presently recognized it as that of Usher. In an instant afterward he rapped, with a gentle touch, at my door, and entered, bearing a lamp. His countenance was, as usual, cadaverously wan—but, moreover, there was a species of mad hilarity in his eyes—an evidently restrained *hysteria* in his whole demeanor. His air appalled me—but anything was preferable to the solitude which I had so long endured, and I even welcomed his presence as a relief.

33   "And you have not seen it?" he said abruptly, after having stared about him for some moments in silence—"you have not then seen it?—but, stay! you shall." Thus speaking, and having carefully shaded his lamp, he hurried to one of the casements, and threw it freely open to the storm.

34   The impetuous fury of the entering gust nearly lifted us from our feet. It was, indeed, a tempestuous yet sternly beautiful night, and one wildly singular in its terror and its beauty. A whirlwind had apparently collected its force in our vicinity; for there were frequent and violent alterations in the direction of the wind; and the exceeding density of the clouds (which hung so low as to press upon the turrets of the house) did not prevent our perceiving the life-like velocity with which they flew careering from all points against each other, without passing away into the distance. I say that even their exceeding density did not prevent our perceiving this—yet we had no glimpse of the moon or stars, nor was there any flashing forth of the lightning. But the under surfaces of the huge masses of agitated vapor, as well as all terrestrial objects immediately around us, were glowing in the unnatural light of a faintly luminous and distinctly visible gaseous exhalation which hung about and enshrouded the mansion.

35   "You must not—you shall not behold this!" said I, shuddering, to Usher, as I led him, with a gentle violence, from the window to a seat. "These appearances, which bewilder you, are merely electrical phenomena not uncommon—or it may be that they have their ghastly origin in the rank miasma of the tarn. Let us close this casement;—the air is chilling and dangerous to your frame. Here is one of your favorite romances. I will read, and you shall listen:—and so we will pass away this terrible night together."

36 The antique volume which I had taken up was the "Mad Trist" of Sir Launcelot Canning;[6] but I had called it a favorite of Usher's more in sad jest than in earnest; for, in truth, there is little in its uncouth and unimaginative prolixity which could have had interest for the lofty and spiritual ideality of my friend. It was, however, the only book immediately at hand; and I indulged a vague hope that the excitement which now agitated the hypochondriac, might find relief (for the history of mental disorder is full of similar anomalies) even in the extremeness of the folly which I should read. Could I have judged, indeed, by the wild overstrained air of vivacity with which he hearkened, or apparently hearkened, to the words of the tale, I might well have congratulated myself upon the success of my design.

37 I had arrived at that well-known portion of the story where Ethelred, the hero of the Trist, having sought in vain for peaceable admission into the dwelling of the hermit, proceeds to make good an entrance by force. Here, it will be remembered, the words of the narrative run thus:

38 "And Ethelred, who was by nature of a doughty heart, and who was now mighty withal, on account of the powerfulness of the wine which he had drunken, waited no longer to hold parley with the hermit, who, in sooth, was of an obstinate and maliceful turn, but, feeling the rain upon his shoulders, and fearing the rising of the tempest, uplifted his mace outright, and, with blows, made quickly room in the plankings of the door for his gauntleted hand; and now pulling therewith sturdily, he so cracked, and ripped, and tore all asunder, that the noise of the dry and hollow-sounding wood alarumed and reverberated throughout the forest."

39 At the termination of this sentence I started and, for a moment, paused; for it appeared to me (although I at once concluded that my excited fancy had deceived me)—it appeared to me that, from some very remote portion of the mansion, there came, indistinctly to my ears, what might have been, in its exact similarity of character, the echo (but a stifled and dull one certainly) of the very cracking and ripping sound which Sir Launcelot had so particularly described. It was, beyond doubt, the coincidence alone which had arrested my attention; for, amid the rattling of the sashes of the casements,[7] and the ordinary commingled noises of the still increasing storm, the sound, in itself, had nothing, surely, which should have interested or disturbed me. I continued the story:

40 "But the good champion Ethelred, now entering within the door, was sore enraged and amazed to perceive no signal of the maliceful hermit; but, in the stead thereof, a dragon of a scaly and prodigious demeanor, and of a fiery

---

6. **"Mad Trist" of Sir Launcelot Canning** a work of fiction written by Poe, which he attributed to Sir Launcelot Canning, who is also fictitious
7. **casements** hinged windows

tongue, which sate in guard before a palace of gold, with a floor of silver; and upon the wall there hung a shield of shining brass with this legend enwritten—

41   Who entereth herein, a conqueror hath bin;
     Who slayeth the dragon, the shield he shall win.

42   And Ethelred uplifted his mace, and struck upon the head of the dragon, which fell before him, and gave up his pesty breath, with a shriek so horrid and harsh, and withal so piercing, that Ethelred had fain to close his ears with his hands against the dreadful noise of it, the like whereof was never before heard."

43   Here again I paused abruptly, and now with a feeling of wild amazement—for there could be no doubt whatever that, in this instance, I did actually hear (although from what direction it proceeded I found it impossible to say) a low and apparently distant, but harsh, protracted, and most unusual screaming or grating sound—the exact counterpart of what my fancy had already conjured up for the dragon's unnatural shriek as described by the romancer.

44   Oppressed, as I certainly was, upon the occurrence of this second and most extraordinary coincidence, by a thousand conflicting sensations, in which wonder and extreme terror were predominant, I still retained sufficient presence of mind to avoid exciting, by any observation, the sensitive nervousness of my companion. I was by no means certain that he had noticed the sounds in question; although, assuredly, a strange alteration had, during the last few minutes, taken place in his demeanor. From a position fronting my own, he had gradually brought round his chair, so as to sit with his face to the door of the chamber; and thus I could but partially perceive his features, although I saw that his lips trembled as if he were murmuring inaudibly. His head had dropped upon his breast—yet I knew that he was not asleep, from the wide and rigid opening of the eye as I caught a glance of it in profile. The motion of his body, too, was at variance with this idea—for he rocked from side to side with a gentle yet constant and uniform sway. Having rapidly taken notice of all this, I resumed the narrative of Sir Launcelot, which thus proceeded:

45   "And now, the champion, having escaped from the terrible fury of the dragon, bethinking himself of the brazen shield, and of the breaking up of the enchantment which was upon it, removed the carcass from out of the way before him, and approached valorously over the silver pavement of the castle to where the shield was upon the wall; which in sooth tarried not for his full coming, but fell down at his feet upon the silver floor, with a mighty great and terrible ringing sound."

46   No sooner had these syllables passed my lips, than—as if a shield of brass had indeed, at the moment, fallen heavily upon a floor of silver—I became

aware of a distinct, hollow, metallic, and clangorous, yet apparently muffled, reverberation. Completely unnerved, I leaped to my feet; but the measured rocking movement of Usher was undisturbed. I rushed to the chair in which he sat. His eyes were bent fixedly before him, and throughout his whole countenance there reigned a stony rigidity. But, as I placed my hand upon his shoulder, there came a strong shudder over his whole person; a sickly smile quivered about his lips; and I saw that he spoke in a low, hurried, and gibbering murmur, as if unconscious of my presence. Bending closely over him, I at length drank in the hideous import of his words.

47 "Not hear it?—yes, I hear it, and *have* heard it. Long—long—long—many minutes, many hours, many days, have I heard it—yet I dared not—oh, pity me, miserable wretch that I am!—I dared not—I *dared* not speak! *We have put her living in the tomb!* Said I not that my senses were acute? I *now* tell you that I heard her first feeble movements in the hollow coffin. I heard them—many, many days ago—yet I dared not—*I dared not speak!* And now—to-night—Ethelred—ha! ha!—the breaking of the hermit's door, and the death-cry of the dragon, and the clangor of the shield!—say, rather, the rending of her coffin, and the grating of the iron hinges of her prison, and her struggles within the coppered archway of the vault! Oh! whither shall I fly? Will she not be here anon? Is she not hurrying to upbraid me for my haste? Have I not heard her footstep on the stair? Do I not distinguish that heavy and horrible beating of her heart? Madman!"—here he sprang furiously to his feet, and shrieked out his syllables, as if in the effort he were giving up his soul—*"Madman! I tell you that she now stands without the door!"*

48 As if in the superhuman energy of his utterance there had been found the potency of a spell, the huge antique panels to which the speaker pointed threw slowly back, upon the instant, their ponderous and ebony jaws. It was the work of the rushing gust—but then without those doors there *did* stand the lofty and enshrouded figure of the lady Madeline of Usher. There was blood upon her white robes, and the evidence of some bitter struggle upon every portion of her emaciated frame. For a moment she remained trembling and reeling to and fro upon the threshold—then, with a low moaning cry, fell heavily inward upon the person of her brother, and in her violent and now final death-agonies, bore him to the floor a corpse, and a victim to the terrors he had anticipated.

49 From that chamber, and from that mansion, I fled aghast. The storm was still abroad in all its wrath as I found myself crossing the old causeway. Suddenly there shot along the path a wild light, and I turned to see whence a gleam so unusual could have issued; for the vast house and its shadows were alone behind me. The radiance was that of the full, setting, and blood-red moon which now shone vividly through that once barely-discernible fissure of which I have before spoken as extending from the roof of the building, in a zigzag

direction, to the base. While I gazed, this fissure rapidly widened—there came a fierce breath of the whirlwind—the entire orb of the satellite burst at once upon my sight—my brain reeled as I saw the mighty walls rushing asunder—there was a long tumultuous shouting sound like the voice of a thousand waters—and the deep and dank tarn at my feet closed sullenly and silently over the fragments of the "*House of Usher.*"

✏️ WRITE

EXPLANATORY: In many horror stories and horror movies, a house serves as a symbol, and some may even consider the house a character. How is the house described in "The Fall of the House of Usher"? What does it symbolize? How does the house itself define the people who live in it? Why are houses that are haunted, dilapidated, or mysterious so common in the horror genre? Support your explanation using evidence from the text and original commentary.

In Our Neighborhood

FICTION
Alice Dunbar-Nelson
1895

Introduction

Alice Dunbar-Nelson (1875–1935) was born in New Orleans to mixed-race parents. Moving easily between genres, she was a journalist, poet, essayist, diarist, and short story writer. As a woman with African American, Caucasian, Native American, and Creole heritage, she wrote elegantly about the complexities of issues such as racism, family, community, gender, ethnicity, and sexuality. "In Our Neighborhood," from Dunbar-Nelson's first book of stories, *Violets and Other Tales*, is a good example of her sure feel for the ironic nuances of a Southern neighborhood.

"The Harts were going to give a party."

1 The Harts were going to give a party. Neither Mrs. Hart, nor the Misses Hart, nor the small and busy Harts who amused themselves and the neighborhood by continually falling in the gutter on special occasions, had mentioned this fact to anyone, but all the interested denizens of that particular square could tell by the unusual air of bustle and activity which pervaded the Hart **domicile**. Lillian, the æsthetic,[1] who furnished theme for many spirited discussions, leaned airily out of the window; her auburn (red) tresses carefully done in curl papers. Martha, the practical, flourished the broom and duster with unwonted activity, which the small boys of the neighborhood, peering through the green shutters of the front door, duly reported to their mammas, busily engaged in holding down their respective door-steps by patiently sitting thereon.

2 Pretty soon, the junior Harts,—two in number—began to travel to and fro, soliciting the loan of a "few chairs," "some nice dishes," and such like things, indispensable to every decent, self-respecting party. But to all inquiries as to the use to which these articles were to be put, they only vouchsafed one reply, "Ma told us as we wasn't to tell, just ask for the things, that's all."

3 Mrs. Tuckley the dress-maker, brought her sewing out on the front-steps, and entered a vigorous protest to her next-door neighbor.

4 "Humph," she sniffed, "mighty funny they can't say what's up. Must be something in it. Couldn't get none o' *my* things, and not invite *me*!"

5 "Did she ask you for any?" absent-mindedly inquired Mrs. Luke, shielding her eyes from the sun.

6 "No-o—, but she'd better sense, she knows *me*—she ain't—mercy me, Stella! Just look at that child tumbling in the mud! You, Stella, come here, I say! Look at you now, there—and there—and there?"

7 The luckless Stella having been soundly cuffed, and sent whimpering in the back-yard, Mrs. Tuckley continued, "Yes as I was saying, 'course, taint none o'

---

1. **æsthetic** dated spelling of aesthetic; concerned with beauty or appearance

my business, but I always did wonder how them Harts do keep up. Why, them girls dress just as fine as any lady on the Avenue and that there Lillian wears real diamond ear-rings. 'Pears mighty, mighty funny to me, and Lord the airs they do put on! Holdin' up their heads like nobody's good enough to speak to. I don't like to talk about people, you know, yourself, Mrs. Luke I never speak about anybody, but mark my word, girls that cut up capers like them Hartses' girls never come to any good."

8   Mrs. Luke heaved a deep sigh of appreciation at the wisdom of her neighbor, but before she could reply a re-inforcement in the person of little Mrs. Peters, apron over her head, hands shrivelled and soap-sudsy from washing, appeared.

9   "Did you ever see the like?" she asked in her usual, rapid breathless way. "Why, my Louis says they're putting canvass cloths on the floor, and taking down the bed in the back-room; and putting greenery and such like trash about. Some style about them, eh?"

10 Mrs. Tuckley tossed her head and sniffed contemptuously, Mrs. Luke began to rehearse a time worn tale, how once a carriage had driven up to the Hart house at nine o'clock at night, and a distinguished looking man alighted, went in, stayed about ten minutes and finally drove off with a great clatter. Heads that had shaken ominously over this story before began to shake again, and tongues that had wagged themselves tired with conjectures started now with some brand new ideas and theories. The children of the square, tired of fishing for minnows in the ditches, and making mud-pies in the street, clustered about their mother's skirts receiving occasional slaps, when their attempts at taking part in the conversation became too pronounced.

11 Meanwhile, in the Hart household, all was bustle and preparation. To and fro the members of the house flitted, arranging chairs, putting little touches here and there, washing saucers and glasses, chasing the Hart Juniors about, losing things and calling frantically for each other's assistance to find them. Mama Hart, big, plump and perspiring, puffed here and there like a large, rosy engine, giving impossible orders, and receiving sharp answers to foolish questions. Lillian, the æsthetic, practiced her most graceful poses before the large mirror in the parlor; Martha rushed about, changing the order of the furniture, and Papa Hart, just come in from work, paced the rooms disconsolately, asking for dinner.

12 "Dinner!" screamed Mama Hart, "Dinner, who's got time to fool with dinner this evening? Look in the sideboard and you'll see some bread and ham; eat that and shut up."

13 Eight o'clock finally arrived, and with it, the music and some straggling guests. When the first faint chee-chee of the violin floated out into the murky atmosphere, the smaller portion of the neighborhood went straightway into ecstasies. Boys and girls in all stages of deshabille clustered about the door-steps and gave vent to audible exclamations of approval or disapprobation concerning the state of affairs behind the green shutters. It was a warm night and the big round moon sailed serenely in a cloudless, blue sky. Mrs. Tuckley had put on a clean calico wrapper, and planted herself with the indomitable Stella on her steps, "to watch the purceedings."

14 The party was a grand success. Even the **intensely** critical small fry dancing on the pavement without to the scraping and fiddling of the string band, had to admit that. So far as they were concerned it was all right, but what shall we say of the guests within? They who glided easily over the canvassed floors, bowed, and scraped and simpered, "just like the big folks on the Avenue," who ate the ice-cream and cake, and drank the sweet, weak Catawba wine amid boisterous healths to Mr. and Mrs. Hart and the Misses Hart; who smirked and perspired and cracked ancient jokes and heart-rending puns during the intervals of the dances, who shall say that they did not enjoy themselves as thoroughly and as fully as those who frequented the wealthier entertainments up-town.

15 Lillian and Martha in gossamer gowns of pink and blue flitted to and fro attending to the wants of their guests. Mrs. Hart, gorgeous in a black satin affair, all folds and lace and drapery, made desperate efforts to appear cool and collected—and failed miserably. Papa Hart spent one half his time standing in front of the mantle, spreading out his coat-tails, and **benignly** smiling upon the young people, while the other half was devoted to initiating the male portion of the guests into the mysteries of "snake killing."

16 Everybody had said that he or she had had a splendid time, and finally, when the last kisses had been kissed, the last good-byes been said, the whole Hart family sat down in the now deserted and disordered rooms, and sighed with relief that the great event was over at last.

17 "Nice crowd, eh?" remarked Papa Hart. He was brimful of joy and second-class whiskey, so no one paid any attention to him.

18 "But did you see how shamefully Maude flirted with Willie Howard?" said Lillian. Martha tossed her head in disdain; Mr. Howard she had always considered her especial property, so Lillian's observation had a rather disturbing effect.

19 "I'm so warm and tired," cried Mama Hart, plaintively, "children how are we going to sleep to-night?"

20 Thereupon the whole family arose to devise ways and means for wooing the drowsy god. As for the Hart Juniors they had long since solved the problem by falling asleep with sticky hands and faces upon a pile of bed-clothing behind the kitchen door.

21 It was late in the next day before the house had begun to resume anything like its former appearance. The little Harts were kept busy all morning returning chairs and dishes, and distributing the remnants of the feast to the vicinity. The ice-cream had melted into a warm custard, and the cakes had a rather worse for wear appearance, but they were appreciated as much as though just from the confectioner. No one was forgotten, even Mrs. Tuckley, busily stitching on a muslin garment on the steps, and unctuously rolling the latest morsel of scandal under her tongue, was obliged to confess that "them Hartses wasn't such bad people after all, just a bit queer at times."

22 About two o'clock, just as Lillian was re-draping the tidies on the stiff, common plush chairs in the parlor, some one pulled the bell violently. The visitor, a rather good-looking young fellow, with a worried **expression** smiled somewhat sarcastically as he heard a sound of scuffling and running within the house.

23 Presently Mrs. Hart opened the door wiping her hand, red and smoking with dish-water, upon her apron. The worried expression deepened on the visitor's face as he addressed the woman with visible embarrassment.

24 "Er—I—I—suppose you are Mrs. Hart?" he inquired awkwardly.

25 "That's my name, sir," replied she with pretentious dignity.

26 "Er—your-er—may I come in madam?"

27 "Certainly," and she opened the door to admit him, and offered a chair.

28 "Your husband is an employee in the Fisher Oil Mills, is he not?"

29 Mrs. Hart straightened herself with pride as she replied in the affirmative. She had always been proud of Mr. Hart's position as foreman of the big oil mills, and was never so happy as when he was expounding to someone in her presence, the difficulties and intricacies of machine-work.

30 "Well you see my dear Mrs. Hart," continued the visitor. "Now pray don't get excited—there has been an accident, and your husband—has—er--been hurt, you know."

31 But for a painful whitening in her usually rosy face, and a quick compression of her lips, the wife made no sign.

32 "What was the accident?" she queried, leaning her elbows on her knees.

33 "Well, you see, I don't understand machinery and the like, but there was something about a wheel out of gear, and a band bursted, or something, anyhow a big wheel flew to pieces, and as he was standing near, he was hit."

34 "Where?"

35 "Well—well, I may as well tell you the truth, madam; a large piece of the wheel struck him on the head—and—he was killed instantly."

36 She did not faint, nor make any outcry, nor tear her hair as he had partly expected, but sat still staring at him, with a sort of helpless, dumb horror shining out her eyes, then with a low moan, bowed her head on her knees and shuddered, just as Lillian came in, curious to know what the handsome stranger had to say to her mother.

37 The poor mutilated body came home at last, and was laid in a stiff, silver-decorated, black coffin in the middle of the sitting-room, which had been made to look as uncomfortable and unnatural as mirrors and furniture shrouded in sheets and mantel and tables divested of ornaments would permit.

38 There was a wake that night to the unconfined joy of the neighbors, who would rather a burial than a wedding. The friends of the family sat about the coffin, and through the house with long pulled faces. Mrs. Tuckley officiated in the kitchen, making coffee and dispensing cheese and crackers to those who were hungry. As the night wore on, and the first restraint disappeared, jokes were cracked, and quiet laughter indulged in, while the young folks congregated in the kitchen, were hilariously happy, until some member of the family would appear, when every face would sober down.

39 The older persons contented themselves with recounting the virtues of the deceased, and telling anecdotes wherein he figured largely. It was astonishing how many intimate friends of his had suddenly come to light. Every other man present had either attended school with him, or was a close companion until he died. Proverbs and tales and witty sayings were palmed off as having emanated from his lips. In fact, the dead man would have been surprised

himself, had he suddenly come to life and discovered what an important, what a modern solomon he had become.

40 The long night dragged on, and the people departed in groups of twos and threes, until when the gray dawn crept slowly over the blackness of night shrouding the electric lights in mists of cloudy blue, and sending cold chills of dampness through the house, but a few of the great crowd remained.

41 The day seemed so gray in **contrast** to the softening influence of the night, the grief which could be hidden then, must now come forth and parade itself before all eyes. There was the funeral to prepare for; the dismal black dresses and bonnets with their long crape veils to don; there were the condolences of sorrowing friends to receive; the floral offerings to be looked at. The little Harts strutted about resplendent in stiff black cravats, and high crape bands about their hats. They were divided between two conflicting emotions—joy at belonging to a family so noteworthy and important, and sorrow at the death. As the time for the funeral approached, and Lillian began to indulge in a series of fainting fits, the latter feeling predominated.

42 Well it was all over at last, the family had returned, and as on two nights previous, sat once more in the deserted and dismantled parlor. Mrs. Tuckley and Mrs. Luke, having rendered all assistance possible, had repaired to their respective front steps to keep count of the number of visitors who returned to condole with the family.

43 "A real nice funeral," remarked the dress-maker at last, "a nice funeral. Everybody took it so hard, and Lillian fainted real beautiful. She's a good girl that Lillian. Poor things, I wonder what they'll do now."

44 Stella, the irrepressible, was busily engaged balancing herself on one toe, *a la* ballet.

45 "Mebbe she's goin' to get married," she volunteered eagerly, "'cos I saw that yeller-haired young man what comes there all the time, wif his arms around her waist, and a tellin' her not to grieve as he'd take care of her. I was a peepin' in the dinin'-room."

46 "How dare you peep at other folks, and pry into people's affairs? I can't imagine where you get your meddlesome ways from. There aint none in *my family*. Next time I catch you at it, I'll spank you good." Then, after a pause, "Well what else did he say?"

✏ WRITE

LITERARY ANALYSIS: This story is built around two central events, a party and a funeral. Write an essay analyzing the relationship between the party and the wake. What are the parallels between them? What are the differences? Why do you think the author chose to concentrate on these two events? Be sure to cite specific examples from the text to support your claims.

The Yellow Wallpaper

FICTION
Charlotte Perkins Gilman
1892

Introduction

Charlotte Perkins Gilman (1860–1935) was an American author and social reformer. She wrote her best-known short story, "The Yellow Wallpaper," after being ordered by her own doctor to take a "rest cure" to recover from depression. The result of three months of desperate boredom, Gilman sent it to her doctor as a critique of the sexism in the medical establishment. "The Yellow Wallpaper" follows a sickly wife who has grown bored while on bed rest in the nursery room of a rambling mansion. With a secret journal as her only distraction,

"... these nervous troubles are dreadfully depressing."

Charlotte Perkins Gilman

1. It is very seldom that mere ordinary people like John and myself secure ancestral halls for the summer.

2. A colonial mansion, a hereditary estate, I would say a haunted house, and reach the height of romantic felicity—but that would be asking too much of fate!

3. Still I will proudly declare that there is something queer about it.

4. Else, why should it be let so cheaply? And why have stood so long untenanted?

5. John laughs at me, of course, but one expects that in marriage.

6. John is practical in the extreme. He has no patience with faith, an **intense** horror of superstition, and he scoffs openly at any talk of things not to be felt and seen and put down in figures.

7. John is a physician, and PERHAPS—(I would not say it to a living soul, of course, but this is dead paper and a great relief to my mind)—PERHAPS that is one reason I do not get well faster.

8. You see he does not believe I am sick!

9. And what can one do?

10. If a physician of high standing, and one's own husband, **assures** friends and relatives that there is really nothing the matter with one but temporary nervous depression—a slight hysterical tendency—what is one to do?

11. My brother is also a physician, and also of high standing, and he says the same thing.

12. So I take phosphates or phosphites—whichever it is, and tonics, and journeys, and air, and exercise, and am absolutely forbidden to "work" until I am well again.

13. Personally, I disagree with their ideas.

14. Personally, I believe that congenial work, with excitement and change, would do me good.

15. But what is one to do?

16. I did write for a while in spite of them; but it DOES exhaust me a good deal—having to be so sly about it, or else meet with heavy opposition.

17. I sometimes fancy that in my **condition** if I had less opposition and more society and stimulus—but John says the very worst thing I can do is to think about my condition, and I confess it always makes me feel bad.

18. So I will let it alone and talk about the house.

19. The most beautiful place! It is quite alone, standing well back from the road, quite three miles from the village. It makes me think of English places that you read about, for there are hedges and walls and gates that lock, and lots of separate little houses for the gardeners and people.

20. There is a DELICIOUS garden! I never saw such a garden—large and shady, full of box-bordered paths, and lined with long grape-covered arbors with seats under them.

21. There were greenhouses, too, but they are all broken now.

22. There was some legal trouble, I believe, something about the heirs and coheirs; anyhow, the place has been empty for years.

23. That spoils my ghostliness, I am afraid, but I don't care—there is something strange about the house—I can feel it.

24. I even said so to John one moonlight evening, but he said what I felt was a DRAUGHT, and shut the window.

25. I get unreasonably angry with John sometimes. I'm sure I never used to be so sensitive. I think it is due to this nervous condition.

26. But John says if I feel so, I shall neglect proper self-control; so I take pains to control myself—before him, at least, and that makes me very tired.

27. I don't like our room a bit. I wanted one downstairs that opened on the piazza and had roses all over the window, and such pretty old-fashioned chintz hangings! but John would not hear of it.

28. He said there was only one window and not room for two beds, and no near room for him if he took another.

29. He is very careful and loving, and hardly lets me stir without special direction.

30. I have a schedule prescription for each hour in the day; he takes all care from me, and so I feel basely ungrateful not to value it more.

31. He said we came here solely on my account, that I was to have perfect rest and all the air I could get. "Your exercise depends on your strength, my dear," said he, "and your food somewhat on your appetite; but air you can absorb all the time." So we took the nursery at the top of the house.

32. It is a big, airy room, the whole floor nearly, with windows that look all ways, and air and sunshine galore. It was nursery first and then playroom and gymnasium, I should judge; for the windows are barred for little children, and there are rings and things in the walls.

33. The paint and paper look as if a boys' school had used it. It is stripped off—the paper—in great patches all around the head of my bed, about as far as I can reach, and in a great place on the other side of the room low down. I never saw a worse paper in my life.

34. One of those sprawling flamboyant patterns committing every artistic sin.

35. It is dull enough to confuse the eye in following, pronounced enough to constantly irritate and provoke study, and when you follow the lame uncertain curves for a little distance they suddenly commit suicide—plunge off at outrageous angles, destroy themselves in unheard of contradictions.

36. The color is repellent, almost revolting; a smouldering unclean yellow, strangely faded by the slow-turning sunlight.

37. It is a dull yet lurid orange in some places, a sickly sulphur tint in others.

38. No wonder the children hated it! I should hate it myself if I had to live in this room long. There comes John, and I must put this away,—he hates to have me write a word.

39. We have been here two weeks, and I haven't felt like writing before, since that first day.

The Yellow Wallpaper

NOTES

40 I am sitting by the window now, up in this atrocious nursery, and there is nothing to hinder my writing as much as I please, save lack of strength.

41 John is away all day, and even some nights when his cases are serious.

42 I am glad my case is not serious!

43 But these nervous troubles are dreadfully depressing.

44 John does not know how much I really suffer. He knows there is no REASON to suffer, and that satisfies him.

45 Of course it is only nervousness. It does weigh on me so not to do my duty in any way!

46 I meant to be such a help to John, such a real rest and comfort, and here I am a comparative burden already!

47 Nobody would believe what an effort it is to do what little I am able,—to dress and entertain, and order things.

48 It is fortunate Mary is so good with the baby. Such a dear baby!

49 And yet I CANNOT be with him, it makes me so nervous.

Skill: Connotation and Denotation

The use of the word "fancies" seems to have a negative connotation here. The use of this word in the context suggests that the husband is belittling the wife's requests.

50 I suppose John never was nervous in his life. He laughs at me so about this wall-paper!

51 At first he meant to repaper the room, but afterwards he said that I was letting it get the better of me, and that nothing was worse for a nervous patient than to give way to such fancies.

52 He said that after the wall-paper was changed it would be the heavy bedstead, and then the barred windows, and then that gate at the head of the stairs, and so on.

53 "You know the place is doing you good," he said, "and really, dear, I don't care to **renovate** the house just for a three months' rental."

54 "Then do let us go downstairs," I said, "there are such pretty rooms there."

55 Then he took me in his arms and called me a blessed little goose, and said he would go down to the cellar, if I wished, and have it whitewashed into the bargain.

56 But he is right enough about the beds and windows and things.

57 It is an airy and comfortable room as any one need wish, and, of course, I would not be so silly as to make him uncomfortable just for a whim.

58 I'm really getting quite fond of the big room, all but that horrid paper.

59 Out of one window I can see the garden, those mysterious deepshaded arbors, the riotous old-fashioned flowers, and bushes and gnarly trees.

60 Out of another I get a lovely view of the bay and a little private wharf belonging to the estate. There is a beautiful shaded lane that runs down there from the house. I always fancy I see people walking in these numerous paths and arbors, but John has cautioned me not to give way to fancy in the least. He says that with my imaginative power and habit of story-making, a nervous weakness like mine is sure to lead to all manner of excited fancies, and that I ought to use my will and good sense to check the tendency. So I try.

61 I think sometimes that if I were only well enough to write a little it would relieve the press of ideas and rest me.

62 But I find I get pretty tired when I try.

63 It is so discouraging not to have any advice and companionship about my work. When I get really well, John says we will ask Cousin Henry and Julia down for a long visit; but he says he would as soon put fireworks in my pillow-case as to let me have those stimulating people about now.

64 I wish I could get well faster.

65 But I must not think about that. This paper looks to me as if it KNEW what a vicious influence it had!

66 There is a recurrent spot where the pattern lolls like a broken neck and two bulbous eyes stare at you upside down.

67 I get positively angry with the impertinence of it and the everlastingness. Up and down and sideways they crawl, and those absurd, unblinking eyes are everywhere. There is one place where two breadths didn't match, and the eyes go all up and down the line, one a little higher than the other.

68 I never saw so much expression in an inanimate thing before, and we all know how much expression they have! I used to lie awake as a child and get more entertainment and terror out of blank walls and plain furniture than most children could find in a toy store.

69 I remember what a kindly wink the knobs of our big, old bureau used to have, and there was one chair that always seemed like a strong friend.

70   I used to feel that if any of the other things looked too fierce I could always hop into that chair and be safe.

71   The furniture in this room is no worse than inharmonious, however, for we had to bring it all from downstairs. I suppose when this was used as a playroom they had to take the nursery things out, and no wonder! I never saw such ravages as the children have made here.

72   The wall-paper, as I said before, is torn off in spots, and it sticketh closer than a brother—they must have had perseverance as well as hatred.

73   Then the floor is scratched and gouged and splintered, the plaster itself is dug out here and there, and this great heavy bed which is all we found in the room, looks as if it had been through the wars.

74   But I don't mind it a bit—only the paper.

75   There comes John's sister. Such a dear girl as she is, and so careful of me! I must not let her find me writing.

76   She is a perfect and enthusiastic housekeeper, and hopes for no better profession. I verily believe she thinks it is the writing which made me sick!

77   But I can write when she is out, and see her a long way off from these windows.

78   There is one that commands the road, a lovely shaded winding road, and one that just looks off over the country. A lovely country, too, full of great elms and velvet meadows.

79   This wall-paper has a kind of sub-pattern in a different shade, a particularly irritating one, for you can only see it in certain lights, and not clearly then.

80   But in the places where it isn't faded and where the sun is just so—I can see a strange, provoking, formless sort of figure, that seems to skulk about behind that silly and conspicuous front design.

81   There's sister on the stairs!

82   Well, the Fourth of July is over! The people are gone and I am tired out. John thought it might do me good to see a little company, so we just had mother and Nellie and the children down for a week.

83   Of course I didn't do a thing. Jennie sees to everything now.

84   But it tired me all the same.

85. John says if I don't pick up faster he shall send me to Weir Mitchell in the fall.

86. But I don't want to go there at all. I had a friend who was in his hands once, and she says he is just like John and my brother, only more so!

87. Besides, it is such an undertaking to go so far.

88. I don't feel as if it was worth while to turn my hand over for anything, and I'm getting dreadfully fretful and querulous.

89. I cry at nothing, and cry most of the time.

90. Of course I don't when John is here, or anybody else, but when I am alone.

91. And I am alone a good deal just now. John is kept in town very often by serious cases, and Jennie is good and lets me alone when I want her to.

92. So I walk a little in the garden or down that lovely lane, sit on the porch under the roses, and lie down up here a good deal.

93. I'm getting really fond of the room in spite of the wall-paper. Perhaps BECAUSE of the wall-paper.

94. It dwells in my mind so!

95. I lie here on this great immovable bed—it is nailed down, I believe—and follow that pattern about by the hour. It is as good as gymnastics, I assure you. I start, we'll say, at the bottom, down in the corner over there where it has not been touched, and I determine for the thousandth time that I WILL follow that pointless pattern to some sort of a conclusion.

96. I know a little of the principle of design, and I know this thing was not arranged on any laws of radiation, or alternation, or repetition, or symmetry, or anything else that I ever heard of.

97. It is repeated, of course, by the breadths, but not otherwise.

98. Looked at in one way each breadth stands alone, the bloated curves and flourishes—a kind of "debased Romanesque" with delirium tremens—go waddling up and down in isolated columns of fatuity.

99. But, on the other hand, they connect diagonally, and the sprawling outlines run off in great slanting waves of optic horror, like a lot of wallowing seaweeds in full chase.

100 The whole thing goes horizontally, too, at least it seems so, and I exhaust myself in trying to **distinguish** the order of its going in that direction.

101 They have used a horizontal breadth for a frieze, and that adds wonderfully to the confusion.

102 There is one end of the room where it is almost intact, and there, when the crosslights fade and the low sun shines directly upon it, I can almost fancy radiation after all,—the interminable grotesques seem to form around a common centre and rush off in headlong plunges of equal distraction.

103 It makes me tired to follow it. I will take a nap I guess.

104 I don't know why I should write this.

105 I don't want to.

106 I don't feel able.

107 And I know John would think it absurd. But I MUST say what I feel and think in some way—it is such a relief!

108 But the effort is getting to be greater than the relief.

109 Half the time now I am awfully lazy, and lie down ever so much.

110 John says I musn't lose my strength, and has me take cod liver oil and lots of tonics and things, to say nothing of ale and wine and rare meat.

111 Dear John! He loves me very dearly, and hates to have me sick. I tried to have a real earnest reasonable talk with him the other day, and tell him how I wish he would let me go and make a visit to Cousin Henry and Julia.

112 But he said I wasn't able to go, nor able to stand it after I got there; and I did not make out a very good case for myself, for I was crying before I had finished.

113 It is getting to be a great effort for me to think straight. Just this nervous weakness I suppose.

114 And dear John gathered me up in his arms, and just carried me upstairs and laid me on the bed, and sat by me and read to me till it tired my head.

115 He said I was his darling and his comfort and all he had, and that I must take care of myself for his sake, and keep well.

116 He says no one but myself can help me out of it, that I must use my will and self-control and not let any silly fancies run away with me.

117 There's one comfort, the baby is well and happy, and does not have to occupy this nursery with the horrid wall-paper.

118 If we had not used it, that blessed child would have! What a fortunate escape! Why, I wouldn't have a child of mine, an impressionable little thing, live in such a room for worlds.

119 I never thought of it before, but it is lucky that John kept me here after all, I can stand it so much easier than a baby, you see.

120 Of course I never mention it to them any more—I am too wise,—but I keep watch of it all the same.

121 There are things in that paper that nobody knows but me, or ever will.

122 Behind that outside pattern the dim shapes get clearer every day.

123 It is always the same shape, only very numerous.

124 And it is like a woman stooping down and creeping about behind that pattern. I don't like it a bit. I wonder—I begin to think—I wish John would take me away from here!

125 It is so hard to talk with John about my case, because he is so wise, and because he loves me so.

126 But I tried it last night.

127 It was moonlight. The moon shines in all around just as the sun does.

128 I hate to see it sometimes, it creeps so slowly, and always comes in by one window or another.

129 John was asleep and I hated to waken him, so I kept still and watched the moonlight on that undulating wall-paper till I felt creepy.

130 The faint figure behind seemed to shake the pattern, just as if she wanted to get out.

131 I got up softly and went to feel and see if the paper DID move, and when I came back John was awake.

132 "What is it, little girl?" he said. "Don't go walking about like that—you'll get cold."

133 I though it was a good time to talk, so I told him that I really was not gaining here, and that I wished he would take me away.

134 "Why darling!" said he, "our lease will be up in three weeks, and I can't see how to leave before.

135 "The repairs are not done at home, and I cannot possibly leave town just now. Of course if you were in any danger, I could and would, but you really are better, dear, whether you can see it or not. I am a doctor, dear, and I know. You are gaining flesh and color, your appetite is better, I feel really much easier about you."

136 "I don't weigh a bit more," said I, "nor as much; and my appetite may be better in the evening when you are here, but it is worse in the morning when you are away!"

137 "Bless her little heart!" said he with a big hug, "she shall be as sick as she pleases! But now let's improve the shining hours by going to sleep, and talk about it in the morning!"

138 "And you won't go away?" I asked gloomily.

139 "Why, how can I, dear? It is only three weeks more and then we will take a nice little trip of a few days while Jennie is getting the house ready. Really dear you are better!"

140 "Better in body perhaps—" I began, and stopped short, for he sat up straight and looked at me with such a stern, reproachful look that I could not say another word.

141 "My darling," said he, "I beg of you, for my sake and for our child's sake, as well as for your own, that you will never for one instant let that idea enter your mind! There is nothing so dangerous, so fascinating, to a temperament like yours. It is a false and foolish fancy. Can you not trust me as a physician when I tell you so?"

142 So of course I said no more on that score, and we went to sleep before long. He thought I was asleep first, but I wasn't, and lay there for hours trying to decide whether that front pattern and the back pattern really did move together or separately.

143 On a pattern like this, by daylight, there is a lack of sequence, a defiance of law, that is a constant irritant to a normal mind.

144 The color is hideous enough, and unreliable enough, and infuriating enough, but the pattern is torturing.

145 You think you have mastered it, but just as you get well underway in following, it turns a back-somersault and there you are. It slaps you in the face, knocks you down, and tramples upon you. It is like a bad dream.

146 The outside pattern is a florid arabesque, reminding one of a fungus. If you can imagine a toadstool in joints, an interminable string of toadstools, budding and sprouting in endless convolutions—why, that is something like it.

147 That is, sometimes!

148 There is one marked peculiarity about this paper, a thing nobody seems to notice but myself, and that is that it changes as the light changes.

149 When the sun shoots in through the east window—I always watch for that first long, straight ray—it changes so quickly that I never can quite believe it.

150 That is why I watch it always.

151 By moonlight—the moon shines in all night when there is a moon—I wouldn't know it was the same paper.

152 At night in any kind of light, in twilight, candle light, lamplight, and worst of all by moonlight, it becomes bars! The outside pattern I mean, and the woman behind it is as plain as can be.

153 I didn't realize for a long time what the thing was that showed behind, that dim sub-pattern, but now I am quite sure it is a woman.

154 By daylight she is subdued, quiet. I fancy it is the pattern that keeps her so still. It is so puzzling. It keeps me quiet by the hour.

155 I lie down ever so much now. John says it is good for me, and to sleep all I can.

156 Indeed he started the habit by making me lie down for an hour after each meal.

157 It is a very bad habit I am convinced, for you see I don't sleep.

158 And that cultivates deceit, for I don't tell them I'm awake—O no!

The Yellow Wallpaper

159 The fact is I am getting a little afraid of John.

160 He seems very queer sometimes, and even Jennie has an inexplicable look.

161 It strikes me occasionally, just as a scientific hypothesis,—that perhaps it is the paper!

162 I have watched John when he did not know I was looking, and come into the room suddenly on the most innocent excuses, and I've caught him several times LOOKING AT THE PAPER! And Jennie too. I caught Jennie with her hand on it once.

163 She didn't know I was in the room, and when I asked her in a quiet, a very quiet voice, with the most restrained manner possible, what she was doing with the paper—she turned around as if she had been caught stealing, and looked quite angry—asked me why I should frighten her so!

164 Then she said that the paper stained everything it touched, that she had found yellow smooches on all my clothes and John's, and she wished we would be more careful!

165 Did not that sound innocent? But I know she was studying that pattern, and I am determined that nobody shall find it out but myself!

166 Life is very much more exciting now than it used to be. You see I have something more to expect, to look forward to, to watch. I really do eat better, and am more quiet than I was.

167 John is so pleased to see me improve! He laughed a little the other day, and said I seemed to be flourishing in spite of my wall-paper.

168 I turned it off with a laugh. I had no intention of telling him it was BECAUSE of the wall-paper—he would make fun of me. He might even want to take me away.

169 I don't want to leave now until I have found it out. There is a week more, and I think that will be enough.

170 I'm feeling ever so much better! I don't sleep much at night, for it is so interesting to watch developments; but I sleep a good deal in the daytime.

171 In the daytime it is tiresome and perplexing.

172 There are always new shoots on the fungus, and new shades of yellow all over it. I cannot keep count of them, though I have tried conscientiously.

173 It is the strangest yellow, that wall-paper! It makes me think of all the yellow things I ever saw—not beautiful ones like buttercups, but old foul, bad yellow things.

174 But there is something else about that paper—the smell! I noticed it the moment we came into the room, but with so much air and sun it was not bad. Now we have had a week of fog and rain, and whether the windows are open or not, the smell is here.

175 It creeps all over the house.

176 I find it hovering in the dining-room, skulking in the parlor, hiding in the hall, lying in wait for me on the stairs.

177 It gets into my hair.

178 Even when I go to ride, if I turn my head suddenly and surprise it—there is that smell!

179 Such a peculiar odor, too! I have spent hours in trying to analyze it, to find what it smelled like.

180 It is not bad—at first, and very gentle, but quite the subtlest, most enduring odor I ever met.

181 In this damp weather it is awful, I wake up in the night and find it hanging over me.

182 It used to disturb me at first. I thought seriously of burning the house—to reach the smell.

183 But now I am used to it. The only thing I can think of that it is like is the COLOR of the paper! A yellow smell.

184 There is a very funny mark on this wall, low down, near the mopboard. A streak that runs round the room. It goes behind every piece of furniture, except the bed, a long, straight, even SMOOCH, as if it had been rubbed over and over.

185 I wonder how it was done and who did it, and what they did it for. Round and round and round—round and round and round—it makes me dizzy!

186 I really have discovered something at last.

187 Through watching so much at night, when it changes so, I have finally found out.

Skill: Connotation and Denotation

Words like "hovering" and "hiding" that often have a neutral connotation take on a more negative connotation here when paired with words like "creeps" and "skulking." Together these words create a sense of fear.

188 The front pattern DOES move—and no wonder! The woman behind shakes it!

189 Sometimes I think there are a great many women behind, and sometimes only one, and she crawls around fast, and her crawling shakes it all over.

190 Then in the very bright spots she keeps still, and in the very shady spots she just takes hold of the bars and shakes them hard.

191 And she is all the time trying to climb through. But nobody could climb through that pattern—it strangles so; I think that is why it has so many heads.

192 They get through, and then the pattern strangles them off and turns them upside down, and makes their eyes white!

193 If those heads were covered or taken off it would not be half so bad.

194 I think that woman gets out in the daytime!

195 And I'll tell you why—privately—I've seen her!

196 I can see her out of every one of my windows!

197 It is the same woman, I know, for she is always creeping, and most women do not creep by daylight.

198 I see her on that long road under the trees, creeping along, and when a carriage comes she hides under the blackberry vines.

199 I don't blame her a bit. It must be very humiliating to be caught creeping by daylight!

200 I always lock the door when I creep by daylight. I can't do it at night, for I know John would suspect something at once.

201 And John is so queer now, that I don't want to irritate him. I wish he would take another room! Besides, I don't want anybody to get that woman out at night but myself.

202 I often wonder if I could see her out of all the windows at once.

203 But, turn as fast as I can, I can only see out of one at one time.

204 And though I always see her, she MAY be able to creep faster than I can turn!

205 I have watched her sometimes away off in the open country, creeping as fast as a cloud shadow in a high wind.

206 If only that top pattern could be gotten off from the under one! I mean to try it, little by little.

207 I have found out another funny thing, but I shan't tell it this time! It does not do to trust people too much.

208 There are only two more days to get this paper off, and I believe John is beginning to notice. I don't like the look in his eyes.

209 And I heard him ask Jennie a lot of professional questions about me. She had a very good report to give.

210 She said I slept a good deal in the daytime.

211 John knows I don't sleep very well at night, for all I'm so quiet!

212 He asked me all sorts of questions, too, and pretended to be very loving and kind.

213 As if I couldn't see through him!

214 Still, I don't wonder he acts so, sleeping under this paper for three months.

215 It only interests me, but I feel sure John and Jennie are secretly affected by it.

216 Hurrah! This is the last day, but it is enough. John is to stay in town over night, and won't be out until this evening.

217 Jennie wanted to sleep with me—the sly thing! but I told her I should undoubtedly rest better for a night all alone.

218 That was clever, for really I wasn't alone a bit! As soon as it was moonlight and that poor thing began to crawl and shake the pattern, I got up and ran to help her.

219 I pulled and she shook, I shook and she pulled, and before morning we had peeled off yards of that paper.

220 A strip about as high as my head and half around the room.

221 And then when the sun came and that awful pattern began to laugh at me, I declared I would finish it to-day!

222 We go away to-morrow, and they are moving all my furniture down again to leave things as they were before.

The Yellow Wallpaper

223 Jennie looked at the wall in amazement, but I told her merrily that I did it out of pure spite at the vicious thing.

224 She laughed and said she wouldn't mind doing it herself, but I must not get tired.

225 How she betrayed herself that time!

226 But I am here, and no person touches this paper but me—not ALIVE!

227 She tried to get me out of the room—it was too patent! But I said it was so quiet and empty and clean now that I believed I would lie down again and sleep all I could; and not to wake me even for dinner—I would call when I woke.

228 So now she is gone, and the servants are gone, and the things are gone, and there is nothing left but that great bedstead nailed down, with the canvas mattress we found on it.

229 We shall sleep downstairs to-night, and take the boat home to-morrow.

230 I quite enjoy the room, now it is bare again.

231 How those children did tear about here!

232 This bedstead is fairly gnawed!

233 But I must get to work.

234 I have locked the door and thrown the key down into the front path.

235 I don't want to go out, and I don't want to have anybody come in, till John comes.

236 I want to astonish him.

237 I've got a rope up here that even Jennie did not find. If that woman does get out, and tries to get away, I can tie her!

238 But I forgot I could not reach far without anything to stand on!

239 This bed will NOT move!

240 I tried to lift and push it until I was lame, and then I got so angry I bit off a little piece at one corner—but it hurt my teeth.

241 Then I peeled off all the paper I could reach standing on the floor. It sticks horribly and the pattern just enjoys it! All those strangled heads and bulbous eyes and waddling fungus growths just shriek with derision!

242 I am getting angry enough to do something desperate. To jump out of the window would be admirable exercise, but the bars are too strong even to try.

243 Besides I wouldn't do it. Of course not. I know well enough that a step like that is improper and might be misconstrued.

244 I don't like to LOOK out of the windows even—there are so many of those creeping women, and they creep so fast.

245 I wonder if they all come out of that wall-paper as I did?

246 But I am securely fastened now by my well-hidden rope—you don't get ME out in the road there!

247 I suppose I shall have to get back behind the pattern when it comes night, and that is hard!

248 It is so pleasant to be out in this great room and creep around as I please!

249 I don't want to go outside. I won't, even if Jennie asks me to.

250 For outside you have to creep on the ground, and everything is green instead of yellow.

251 But here I can creep smoothly on the floor, and my shoulder just fits in that long smooch around the wall, so I cannot lose my way.

252 Why there's John at the door!

253 It is no use, young man, you can't open it!

254 How he does call and pound!

255 Now he's crying for an axe.

256 It would be a shame to break down that beautiful door!

257 "John dear!" said I in the gentlest voice, "the key is down by the front steps, under a plantain leaf!"

258 That silenced him for a few moments.

259 Then he said—very quietly indeed, "Open the door, my darling!"

260 "I can't," said I. "The key is down by the front door under a plantain leaf!"

261 And then I said it again, several times, very gently and slowly, and said it so often that he had to go and see, and he got it of course, and came in. He stopped short by the door.

262 "What is the matter?" he cried. "For God's sake, what are you doing!"

263 I kept on creeping just the same, but I looked at him over my shoulder.

264 "I've got out at last," said I, "in spite of you and Jane. And I've pulled off most of the paper, so you can't put me back!"

265 Now why should that man have fainted? But he did, and right across my path by the wall, so that I had to creep over him every time!

The Yellow Wallpaper

First Read

Read "The Yellow Wallpaper." After you read, complete the Think Questions below.

THINK QUESTIONS

1. What is John's opinion of his wife? Use examples from the text to support your answer.

2. How does the protagonist's mental state change throughout the story? Answer using examples from the text.

3. How do the descriptions of the wallpaper alter as the story goes on? Use examples from the text in your answer.

4. Use context clues to determine the meaning of the word **condition** as it is used in "The Yellow Wallpaper." Write your definition of *condition* here, and explain how you figured it out. Then look up the word in a dictionary and check your definition.

5. Use context clues to determine the meaning of **distinguish**. Then look up the word in a dictionary, and compare your definition with the official definition. Write the definition of *distinguish* here.

The Yellow Wallpaper

Skill:
Connotation and Denotation

Use the Checklist to analyze Connotation and Denotation in "The Yellow Wallpaper." Refer to the sample student annotations about Connotation and Denotation in the text.

••• CHECKLIST FOR CONNOTATION AND DENOTATION

In order to identify the denotative meanings of words, use the following steps:

- ✓ first, note unfamiliar words and phrases, key words used to describe important characters, events, and ideas, or words that inspire an emotional reaction

- ✓ next, determine and note the denotative meaning of words by consulting a reference material such as a dictionary, glossary, or thesaurus

- ✓ finally, analyze nuances in the meaning of words with similar denotations

To better understand the meaning of words and phrases as they are used in a text, including connotative meanings, use the following questions as a guide:

- ✓ What is the genre or subject of the text? Based on context, what do you think the meaning of the word is intended to be?

- ✓ Is your inference the same as or different from the dictionary definition?

- ✓ Does the word create a positive, negative, or neutral emotion?

- ✓ What synonyms or alternative phrasings help you describe the connotative meaning of the word?

To determine the meaning of words and phrases as they are used in a text, including connotative meanings, use the following questions as a guide:

- ✓ What is the denotative meaning of the word? Is that denotative meaning correct in context?

- ✓ What possible positive, neutral, or negative connotations might the word have, depending on context?

- ✓ What textual details signal a particular connotation for the word?

Skill: Connotation and Denotation

Reread paragraphs 59–70 of "The Yellow Wallpaper." Then, using the Checklist on the previous page, answer the multiple-choice questions below.

YOUR TURN

1. Does the protagonist's description of the gardens in the first sentence provide a positive or negative connotation overall?

   ○ A. Overall, the description has a positive connotation due to words such as *garden*, *arbors*, and *flowers*.
   ○ B. Overall, the description has a positive connotation due to words such as *mysterious*, *riotous*, and *gnarly*.
   ○ C. Overall, the description has a negative connotation due to words such as *garden*, *arbors*, and *flowers*.
   ○ D. Overall, the description has a negative connotation due to words such as *mysterious*, *riotous*, and *gnarly*.

2. Which word does not have a positive connotation as used in this excerpt of the text?

   ○ A. entertainment
   ○ B. wink
   ○ C. impertinence
   ○ D. hop

The Yellow Wallpaper

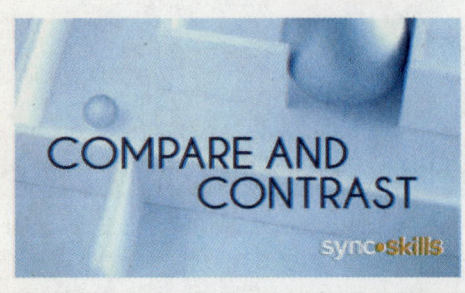

Skill:
Compare and Contrast

Use the Checklist to analyze Compare and Contrast in "The Yellow Wallpaper." Refer to the sample student annotations about Compare and Contrast in the text.

••• CHECKLIST FOR COMPARE AND CONTRAST

In order to determine how to compare and contrast texts from the same period, and how these texts treat similar themes or topics, use the following steps:

- ✓ first, identify two or more foundational works of American literature written during the eighteenth-, nineteenth- or early-twentieth-century

- ✓ next, identify the topic and theme in each work, and any central or recurring topics that each author presents

- ✓ after, explain how each text reflects and represents the time period in which it was written, including its historical events, customs, beliefs, or social norms

- ✓ finally, explain the similarities or differences between each of the texts written during the same time period including how they address related themes and topics

To demonstrate knowledge of and compare and contrast eighteenth-, nineteenth- and early-twentieth-century foundational works of American literature, consider the following questions:

- ✓ Are the texts from the same time period in American literature?

- ✓ In what ways does each text reflect and represent the time period in which it was written?

- ✓ How does each work treat themes or topics representative of the time period in which it was written?

- ✓ How is the treatment of the themes or topics in these literary works similar and different?

The Yellow Wallpaper

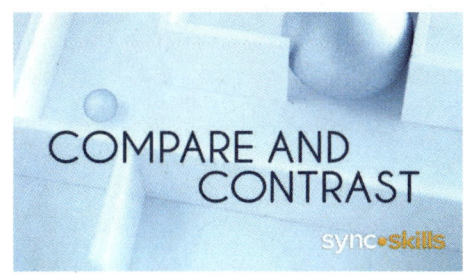

Skill:
Compare and Contrast

Reread paragraphs 104–120 from "The Yellow Wallpaper" and paragraphs 14–16 from "In Our Neighborhood." Then, using the Checklist on the previous page, answer the multiple-choice questions below.

YOUR TURN

1. This question has two parts. First, answer Part A. Then, answer Part B.

   Part A: How are themes regarding the importance of identity explored differently in each text?

   - A. In "The Yellow Wallpaper" the narrator tries to create an identity by writing while the Harts are attempting to maintain an identity of being from a higher social class.
   - B. In "The Yellow Wallpaper" the narrator fights with her husband to maintain her identity while the Harts are attempting to portray an image of being richer than they are.
   - C. In "The Yellow Wallpaper" the narrator tries to create an identity by bonding with her baby while the Harts are attempting to create an image of being able to throw a great party.
   - D. In "The Yellow Wallpaper" the narrator struggles to maintain her identity while under the oppressive care of her husband while the Harts are attempting to create an identity of being from a higher social class.

   Part B: Which lines from the passage from "The Yellow Wallpaper" best support your answer to Part A?

   - A. "And dear John gathered me up in his arms, and just carried me upstairs and laid me on the bed, and sat by me and read to me till it tired my head."
   - B. "And I know John would think it absurd. But I MUST say what I feel and think in some way—it is such a relief!"
   - C. "John says I musn't lose my strength, and has me take cod liver oil and lots of tonics and things, to say nothing of ale and wine and rare meat."
   - D. "I tried to have a real earnest reasonable talk with him the other day, and tell him how I wish he would let me go and make a visit to Cousin Henry and Julia."

Close Read

Reread "The Yellow Wallpaper." As you reread, complete the Skills Focus questions below. Then use your answers and annotations from the questions to help you complete the Write activity.

SKILLS FOCUS

1. Identify when the narrator first describes the yellow wallpaper. What connotations do the words she uses have, and how do these words reveal her attitude towards the wallpaper?

2. Establishing and maintaining one's identity is a common theme in literature from this time period. How does the narrator seek to maintain her identity? To what extent is she successful? Identify evidence from the text to support your answer.

3. Towards the end of the story, the narrator mentions creeping women. Whom might they represent? What connection does she have to them? Identify evidence to support your answer.

4. Themes regarding overcoming societal challenges were common during this literary period. What challenge does the narrator overcome? Find evidence of this at the end of the story.

5. The narrator has a strange relationship with her "home" in this story. How does the narrator's temporary home begin to feel more like a prison? Identify textual evidence to support your answer.

WRITE

COMPARE AND CONTRAST: At the end of the 19th century, themes regarding identity were predominant in American literature. Compare and contrast how each author approaches themes regarding identity in both "In Our Neighborhood" and "The Yellow Wallpaper." Discuss the ways by which the narrator in "The Yellow Wallpaper" and the characters in "In Our Neighborhood" attempt to shape or maintain their identities. Support your response with evidence from the text.

Boyhood

DRAMA
Richard Linklater
2014

Introduction

In 2014, more than a century into the history of motion pictures, director Richard Linklater (b. 1960) did something entirely new. He released a fictional narrative covering 12 years of a boy's life using the same actors. Instead of casting children of different ages who looked alike, Linklater shot the film for two weeks every year—over more than a decade—to imitate real time. The result was a film that incorporated news and pop culture as it happened but also tracked the subtler changes in its child, teen, and adult actors over time. *Boyhood* was nominated for six Oscars including Best Screenplay and Best Picture, and won the prize for Best Supporting Actress for Patricia Arquette. In an excerpt from the screenplay, we observe teenage Mason and his dad on one of their twice-a-month reunions, a narrow window of opportunity for the father to offer guidance and support, and for Mason to seek his help with the mysteries of life.

"Guy's got to be responsible. What do you think?"

INT. MOVING CAR - DAY

1 Dad and Mason are driving along the open road, listening to a song by Wilco.

DAD
2 Now . . . listen to this song, alright?

3 Sings along:

DAD (CONT'D)
4 "I try to stay busy." It's just straight up, the lyrics . . . it's a straight up old school country song.

SONG
5 "I do the dishes, I mow the lawn . . ."

DAD
6 Listen to the **production** of this. Production's like uh, like "Abbey Road" or something.

SONG
7 "I try to keep myself **occupied.**"

8 Dad sings along.

DAD
9 "Even though I know you're not comin' home." You know, his old woman's gone . . . straight up. Nothin' fancy.

DAD AND SONG
10 "I try to keep the house nice and neat. Make my bed. I change the sheets."

EXT. RIVERBED - DAY

11 Mason and Dad walk along the rocks, mid-conversation. They sit down near the water and begin taking off socks and shoes.

	MASON
12	Yeah, I think she's about to get her master's **degree.**

	DAD
13	Well, then she's gonna start applying for teaching jobs?

	MASON
14	I think she already has.

	DAD
15	Really? Where?

	MASON
	(shrugs)
16	All over.

	DAD
17	All over Texas?

	MASON
18	Yeah.

	DAD
19	Well, if you gotta move, you gotta move, you know? It's no big deal. We can handle that. I'll still come get you every other weekend. I mean, unless she moves 500 miles away or something, it'll just be a little more car time. No big deal.

	MASON
20	I'm just kinda sick of moving.

	DAD
21	Well, I bet you are. But you know, you never know. I mean, I might have to move, right? I'm working for this insurance company now. These places get bought and sold all the time. You know? We'll just roll with it.

22 They take off pants, walk up to the water in boxer shorts.

	MASON
23	I thought you were a musician?

	DAD
24	I am but . . . life is expensive, you know. Guy's got to be responsible. What do you think?

25 Mason pushes his Dad into the water, then dives in himself.

Skill: Media

Mason "shrugs" and acts casual about his moving away, but in the video clip I notice he tries to avoid eye contact and his tone of voice is too offhanded. Because of the video, I see that Mason is trying to conceal his sadness.

DAD (CONT'D)
Hey, hey, you bast — Oh you, punk kid!

You got no respect!

Dad splashes his son and they both begin to swim.

. . .

DAD
(back to Mason)
I guarantee you, you didn't do anything wrong. These high school love things, they never work out. Here, come here.

(MORE)

I mean, everyone's just changing so much. The odds of two young people staying on the same wavelength are . . .

MASON
Yeah, but still--

DAD
Look, and I also guarantee you that every day of your life that you spend crying over some silly girl is a complete waste of time.

MASON
She wasn't a silly girl, though. I mean, she's a serious person. I really thought we were—

DAD
What?

MASON
I don't know.

DAD
Here's the truth. Women are never satisfied. Ok? They're always looking to potentially trade up and that's, I'm sorry to say, what I think has happened to you, my fine-feathered friend.

MASON
What does that even mean?

DAD
It means don't hand over the controls to your self-esteem to Sheila.

MASON
38 Sheena.

DAD
39 Alright. It means you are responsible for you, not your girlfriend, your mom, not me. You. And if you truly take care of you, you will be amazed at how much girls like Sheena start lining up at your front door.

MASON
40 Great.

DAD
41 Yeah, you know, you just gotta separate yourself from the pack in some way. **Excel** at something, you know, and then you have your pick of the litter when them front-running hussies start sniffing around.

MASON
42 So what you're saying is, I should take up lacrosse.

DAD
43 Exactly. Or you could, you know, start a band. Worked for me a long time ago. I think it's still working for Jimmy. Or you just keep taking pictures.

MASON
44 She hated the pictures I took of her.

DAD
45 Alright. I'm sick to death of her, okay? I only met her a few times and yes she was cute, alright. But, truth be told I always thought she was a little bit, you know, a little bit too square for you. Y'know, not quite the same vibe.

MASON
46 You really thought that?

© 2014 BOYHOOD INC./IFC PRODUCTIONS I, L.L.C.

Boyhood

First Read

Read *Boyhood*. After you read, complete the Think Questions below.

THINK QUESTIONS

1. How often do Mason and his Dad see each other? What is their particular arrangement, and why does it exist? Do possible changes arise? Cite textual evidence from the selection to support your answer.

2. What does Mason's Dad say that clues us in to his level of dedication to their relationship and its current schedule?

3. Do all the scenes included in the excerpt take place in one visit? How do we know if so, and if not, how do we know that? How much time does the excerpt span?

4. Which context clues helped you determine the meaning of the word **production** as the Dad uses it in the screenplay? Write your definition of *production*, and indicate the clues that helped you figure out the meaning of the word.

5. Which context clues helped you determine the meaning of the term **excel** as it is written in the dialogue? Write your definition of *excel*, and indicate the clues that helped you figure out the meaning of the word.

 Reading & Writing Companion

Skill: Media

Use the Checklist to analyze Media in *Boyhood*. Refer to the sample student annotations about Media in the text.

••• CHECKLIST FOR MEDIA

Before analyzing multiple interpretations of a story, drama, or poem, note the following:

- ✓ similarities and differences in types of media, such as the live production of a play as compared to the film version

- ✓ the similarities, differences, and nuances that can occur between the written version of a work and an audio version

- ✓ the different time periods and cultures in which the source material and interpretations were produced

To analyze multiple interpretations of a story, drama, or poem, evaluating how each version interprets the source text, consider the following questions:

- ✓ How does each version or medium interpret the source text? What are the main similarities and differences between the two (or more) versions?

- ✓ How does a media interpretation of a source text influence or change the audience's understanding of the text? Include how ways of accessing the text might affect the reading experience.

- ✓ If each version is from a different time period and/or culture, what does each version reveal about the time period and culture in which it was written? Does information about the time period and culture allow you to make any inferences about the authors' objectives or intentions?

Boyhood

Skill:
Media

Reread paragraphs 21–27 of *Boyhood* and watch the StudySyncTV episode. Then, using the Checklist on the previous page, answer the multiple-choice questions below.

YOUR TURN

1. The interaction of visual and audio media in the video clip is most likely intended to —

   - A. show that Mason has no respect for his father.
   - B. show that Mason and his father are joking around.
   - C. persuade people to treasure time spent with their parents.
   - D. show that Mason's father is disrespectful.

2. How does the video help support the script's message about the significance of Mason's relationship with his father?

   - A. The video clip contains a montage of childhood photographs, visually representing the memories Mason describes in the clip.
   - B. The video clip uses sound effects to convey Mason's sorrow about his parents' divorce.
   - C. The video clip uses audio and visual media to show that Mason and his father can have serious conversations, as well as joke around with each other.
   - D. The video clip uses audio and visual media to show that Mason and his father often have deep, meaningful conversations about the future.

Boyhood

Close Read

Reread *Boyhood*. As you reread, complete the Skills Focus questions below. Then use your answers and annotations from the questions to help you complete the Write activity.

SKILLS FOCUS

1. Identify a stage direction from the middle of the scene when Mason is a child. Watch the first film clip, and see how this stage direction is executed in the film. Then, analyze how the characteristics of the text and media work to effectively convey a message about childhood.

2. Identify a portion of the screenplay in which the dialogue enhances your understanding of the characters' emotions. Explain the inferences you are able to make based on the dialogue.

3. Identify details from the script that reveal that Mason has matured and grown older. Analyze how viewing the film alongside the text helps readers to understand how Mason has transformed from being a child to becoming a young man.

4. In this excerpt, to what extent is Mason's definition of home connected to a place? Who or what represents home for Mason? Identify evidence from the text to support your answer.

WRITE

PERSONAL RESPONSE: Mason struggles to balance his own individuality with what others expect of him. Choose a crucial time from your own life when you felt torn between what you wanted and what others expected of you. Then, write a journal entry describing that experience and how you responded.

Extended Writing Project and Grammar

Research Writing Process: Plan

| PLAN | DRAFT | REVISE | EDIT AND PUBLISH |

The Harlem Renaissance was a period when African-American art and culture began to flourish in mainstream American culture. Poets, musicians, artists, and writers sought to define and explore the African-American experience on African-American terms. What emerged was a proliferation of work that examined the influence of slavery on the lives of black Americans, brought attention to African-American folklore, introduced a context in which to describe black urban life in the North, addressed the impacts of discrimination, and celebrated African-American culture at large. By bringing these issues into the American cultural mainstream, the Harlem Renaissance also laid the groundwork for the burgeoning civil rights movement of the 1940s and 1950s.

WRITING PROMPT

What role do art and culture have in bringing awareness to social issues?

Choose one to two artists or writers, not included in this unit, from the Harlem Renaissance whom you would like to research. For example, you might research a writer who was born in the South but moved to a Northern city, such as Richard Wright. You might choose to focus on the early life of writer Claude McKay, the career of Paul Robeson, or the success of Ma Rainey. Research your chosen topic, and formulate a position on how your subjects' work contributed to gaining greater visibility for African Americans in mainstream culture, how it impacted society, or how your subjects' life experiences impacted their work. Then, write an informative research essay, using textual evidence and source material to support your ideas. Be sure your informative research paper includes the following:

- an introduction
- supporting details from at least three credible sources
- a clear text structure
- a conclusion
- a works cited page

Writing to Sources

As you gather ideas and information from sources, be sure to:

- use evidence from multiple sources, and
- avoid overly relying on one source.

Extended Writing Project and Grammar

Introduction to Informative Research Writing

Research writing, a type of informative writing, examines a topic and conveys ideas by citing and analyzing information from credible sources. Good research papers use textual evidence, including facts, statistics, examples, and details from reliable sources, to provide information about a topic and to support the analysis of complex ideas. Research helps writers not only to discover and confirm facts, but also to draw new conclusions about a topic. The characteristics of research writing include:

- an introduction with a clear thesis statement
- relevant facts, supporting details, and quotations from credible sources
- analysis of the details to explain how they support the thesis
- a clear and logical text structure
- a formal style
- a conclusion that wraps up your ideas
- a works cited page

In addition to these characteristics, writers also carefully narrow the focus of their research by generating research questions and developing a research plan. The research process requires patience as you evaluate the validity and usefulness of sources related to your topic. Researchers develop the skills of locating sources and assessing their appropriateness over time.

As you continue with this Extended Writing Project, you'll receive more instruction and practice in crafting each of the characteristics of informative research writing to create your own research paper.

Extended Writing Project and Grammar

Before you get started on your own informative research paper, read this research paper that one student, Daniela, wrote in response to the writing prompt. As you read the Model, highlight and annotate the features of informative research writing that Daniela included in her essay.

STUDENT MODEL

Post-Reconstruction Blues:

How Gertrude "Ma" Rainey Sang Black Rural Southerners into Popular American Culture

1   Legendary blues vocalist and Harlem Renaissance artist Gertrude "Ma" Rainey, known as the "Mother of Blues," introduced blues music to a mainstream audience, transforming the genre and expanding opportunities for African-American artists. Through lyrical depictions of black Southern life and the complex experiences of African-American women, Rainey's music increased the visibility of a people silenced in popular culture. While less well-known today, Rainey left a legacy that continues to influence musicians and broaden our knowledge of life for African Americans in the post-Reconstruction era.

2   Ma Rainey was born Gertrude Malissa Nix Pridgett on April 26, 1886, in Columbus, Georgia. Rainey possessed a musical talent from a young age and performed in public for the first time at age 14 at the Springer Opera House in Columbus. Soon after, she found her calling singing on tour in vaudeville and African-American minstrel shows. For more than thirty years, Rainey performed in troupes, such as F.S. Wolcott's Rabbit Foot Minstrels and Tolliver's Circus and Musical Extravaganza.

Vaudeville: Ma Rainey's Early Career

3   Ma Rainey used vaudeville and minstrel shows as a platform to showcase her talent and share her life experiences. Originating from minstrel shows, vaudeville became popular at the turn of the century and featured unrelated acts such as singing, dancing, comedy, acrobatics, and magic. While no video recordings of Ma Rainey exist, the memory of her vibrant performances has been passed down through written reviews. According to critic Mary L. Bogumil in *Understanding August Wilson*, Rainey wore "flamboyant" jewelry and costumes and performed in front of a backdrop that featured a

large gramophone design, "which gave the appearance of Ma emerging right from the speaker, issuing from and manifesting the music itself" (qtd. in Timmel). Such extravagant details exemplify the sensational nature of vaudeville shows. Rainey's bold and brilliant stage persona was magnetic. She forced the audience, who were often men, to listen to what she had to say.

4. The variety show format of vaudeville allowed performers to communicate larger themes to the audience. For example, PBS's *American Masters* says of immigrant performers, "Their acts were a form of assimilation, in which they could become active parts of popular culture through representations of their heritage" ("Vaudeville: About Vaudeville"). In other words, immigrant performers used the highly adaptable and entertaining structure of vaudeville to disseminate information about where they came from. Ma Rainey was not an immigrant. However, as an African-American woman, she belonged to a class of citizens who were underrepresented, misunderstood, and discriminated against. Like the immigrants, she used the modes of performance available to her to subvert boundaries and bring the experiences of Southern African-American women into the mainstream ("Vaudeville: About Vaudeville"). That Ma Rainey was also the first woman to include blues music in her act only further illustrates her ability to use this mode of performance to break barriers and convey an important message (Orr).

The Blues: Ma Rainey's Medium

5. The blues played a central part in Rainey's performances. Originating in the South at the turn of the century, blues emerged from such African musical traditions as field hollers, work songs, spirituals, and country string ballads ("What Is the Blues?"). Most blues songs follow a 12-bar structure with an AAB verse pattern where "the first and second lines are repeated, and the third line is a response to them—often with a twist" ("Understanding the 12-Bar Blues"). Blues music tends to explore melancholy topics, such as sadness, desire, and longing. While many of Rainey's songs had a melancholy tone, her music also served to empower women by approaching topics most women could not discuss freely.

6   Ma Rainey's audience easily connected to her songs because her lyrics discussed aspects of everyday life for black rural Southerners as well as her personal experiences. According to William Barlow in *Looking Up at Down*, Rainey's lyrics captured "the southern landscape of African Americans in the Post-Reconstruction era" through "simple, straightforward stories" (qtd. in Biography.com Editors). For example, in 1923, Rainey recorded her own rendition of the traditional boll weevil song, titled "Bo-Weavil Blues." In the first verse, she sang, "Bo-weavil, don't sing them blues no more / Bo-weavil's here, Bo-weavil's everywhere you'll go." A boll weevil is a type of beetle that feeds on cotton plants. Because boll weevils infested cotton crops in the United States in the 1920s, this lyric reflected rural Southern life at the time. Rainey established a call-and-response structure between the first and second verses as she sang, "I'm a lone bo-weavil, been out a great long time / I'm gonna sing these blues to ease the bo-weavil's lonesome mind." Here, she expanded the boll weevil reference to her personal life. Although there were "bo-weavils" "everywhere you'll go," she still felt "lonesome." "Bo-weavils" represented all the men, or potential romantic partners, available to her.

7   Ma Rainey's candid discussion of love was unique to blues artists of her time. She was lonely but also embraced her independence ("I don't want no man to put sugar in my tea."). Rainey's rejection of a male partner was radical, for women in this time period were expected to build their lives around being married and building a family. In *Blues Legacies and Black Feminism*, Angela Davis pointed out that "black women of that era were acknowledging and addressing issues central to contemporary feminist discourse" (Davis 28). Black female blues artists like Ma Rainey were ahead of

their time in terms of asserting their agency. Rainey's performance of this song introduced the idea of liberated black women into the mainstream. Rainey added complexity to this with a twist in the third verse:

> I went downtown and bought me a hat
> I brought it back home, I laid it on the shelf
> Looked at my bed, I'm getting tired of sleeping by myself (Rainey)

Ma Rainey used straightforward phrases to explain how she tried to compensate for her loneliness by purchasing a hat, but it did not help. The expression "tired of sleeping by myself" emphasized her internal conflict. Sleep is the solution for tiredness, just as a relationship should have been the solution for her loneliness. Yet, Rainey preferred her independence. In only twelve lines, she referenced a regional metaphor, discussed the relatable concept of loneliness, and expressed her personal struggles balancing love and freedom.

Ma Rainey and the Mainstream Music Industry

8 Rainey's vocals had a deep and unembellished tone expressing raw emotion that resonated with a wide range of audiences. "The gravelly timbre of her . . . raspy, deep voice" (Orr) as well as her "moaning style" (Timmel) entranced listeners. Her flashy visual representation attracted the attention of the audience. Her measured and gripping delivery kept them waiting for more. Ma Rainey was one of the first professional female blues artists to make a phonograph record. During the Great Migration, blues music spread from the South into other regions of the nation.

THE GREAT MIGRATION
The Migration of African Americans from the American South (1910 - 1970)

By the 1920s, recording labels saw a market for "race records," or music created by and for African Americans. After establishing her career as a touring musician, Ma Rainey recorded over 100 songs with Paramount in the span of 1923 to 1928 (Timmel). However, in 1928 Paramount stopped recording with Rainey after determining that race records like hers were no longer profitable. One could argue that Paramount exploited Ma Rainey for corporate gain. Still, making a phonograph record with Paramount did help Rainey's audience and success grow. Over the course of her career, she performed alongside various bands and other renowned Harlem Renaissance musicians, such as Louis Armstrong and Bessie Smith.

9 In an era when the possibilities for women of color were limited, the "Mother of Blues," Ma Rainey, surpassed expectations by taking advantage of the modes of performance that were available to her to build a long-lasting career. Rainey used the public platforms of vaudeville and recorded music to tell the stories of Southern African Americans during the post-Reconstruction Era. Her lyrics also revealed her own stories and sentiments that are unique to the experiences of black women at that time. Her deeply emotional vocal style appealed to many people. Ma Rainey's blues music demanded recognition through simple portrayals of authenticity. She brought the silenced narratives of African Americans into the scope of mainstream American culture.

Works Cited

Biography.com Editors. "Ma Rainey Biography." *The Biography.com Website*, A&E Television Networks, 27 Apr. 2017, https://www.biography.com/people/ma-rainey-9542413. Accessed 20 Sept. 2018.

Davis, Angela Y. *Blues Legacies and Black Feminism: Gertrude "Ma" Rainey, Bessie Smith, and Billie Holiday. Google Books*. 2nd ed., Vintage Books, 1999.

Orr, N. Lee. "Gertrude 'Ma' Rainey (1886-1939)." 9 May 2003. *New Georgia Encyclopedia*, Georgia State University, 9 Aug. 2018, https://www.georgiaencyclopedia.org/articles/arts-culture/gertrude-ma-rainey-1886-1939. Accessed 20 Sep. 2018.

Rainey, Ma. "Bo-Weavil Blues." *Harry's Blues Lyrics & Tabs Online*, Recorded December 1923, http://blueslyrics.tripod.com/lyrics/ma rainey/bo weavil blues.htm. Accessed 25 Sep. 2018.

Timmel, Lisa. "The Music of Ma Rainey." *Huntington Theater Company*, https://www.huntingtontheatre.org/articles/Ma-Raineys-Black-Bottom/music-ma-rainey/. Accessed 20 Sep. 2018.

"The Great Migration, 1910 to 1970." The United States Census Bureau, September 13, 2012, https://www.census.gov/dataviz/visualizations/020/. Accessed 20 Sep. 2018.

"Understanding the 12-Bar Blues." *PBS: The Blues*, 2003, www.pbs.org/theblues/classroom/essays12bar.html. Accessed 21 Sep. 2018.

"Vaudeville: About Vaudeville." *PBS: American Masters*, 8 Oct. 1999, www.pbs.org/wnet/americanmasters/vaudeville-about-vaudeville/721/. Accessed 20 Sept. 2018.

"What Is the Blues?" *PBS: The Blues*, 2003, www.pbs.org/theblues/classroom/essaysblues.html. Accessed 21 Sep. 2018.

WRITE

Writers often take notes about ideas before they sit down to write. Think about what you've learned so far about organizing informative research writing to help you begin prewriting.

- **Purpose:** Which Harlem Renaissance writer or artist do you find most influential? What do you want to learn about your chosen subject?
- **Audience:** Who is your audience, and what information do you want your audience to learn?
- **Questions:** How can you use a research question to focus your research?
- **Sources:** What kinds of sources will help you answer that question?
- **Structure:** How can you share the information you find with readers?

Response Instructions

Use the questions in the bulleted list to write a one-paragraph research summary. Your summary should describe what you plan to research and discuss in this research paper. Include possible research questions of your own based on the prompt.

Don't worry about including all of the details now; focus only on the most essential and important elements. You will refer to this short summary as you continue through the steps of the writing process.

Skill: Planning Research

••• CHECKLIST FOR PLANNING RESEARCH

In order to conduct a short or more sustained research project to answer a question or solve a problem, do the following:

- select a topic or problem to research
- think about what you want to find out and what kind of research can contribute to the project
- start to formulate your major research question by asking open-ended questions that begin "How . . . ?" and "Why . . . ?" and then choose a question that you are interested in exploring
- narrow or broaden your inquiry when appropriate, sorting information or items into clear categories
- synthesize multiple sources on the subject to look at information from different points of view, while demonstrating understanding of the subject under investigation

In order to conduct a short or more sustained research project to answer a question or solve a problem, consider the following questions:

- Does my major research question allow me to explore a new issue, an important problem worth solving, or a fresh perspective on a topic?
- Can I research my question within my given time frame and with the resources available to me?
- Have I synthesized multiple sources on the question or problem, looking for different points of view?
- Have I demonstrated understanding of the subject under investigation in my research project?

Extended Writing Project and Grammar

YOUR TURN

Read the research questions below. Then, complete the chart by sorting the questions into the correct category. Write the corresponding letter for each question in the appropriate column.

	Research Questions
A	What is Louis Armstrong remembered for?
B	Why did Louis Armstrong specialize in playing the trumpet?
C	How does Nella Larsen's literary work relate to her personal life?
D	What are the events in Nella Larsen's novel *Passing*?
E	How did Louis Armstrong's artistry influence jazz?
F	What was Langston Hughes's poetry about?
G	What beliefs are reflected in Langston Hughes's poetry?
H	Why do people still read Nella Larsen's work today?
I	Who were Langston Hughes's literary inspirations?

Topic	Too Narrow	Appropriate	Too Broad
Louis Armstrong			
Nella Larsen			
Langston Hughes			

Extended Writing Project and Grammar

YOUR TURN

Develop a research question for formal research. Then, write a short plan for how you will go about doing research for your essay. Include a note about how you might need to modify your plan during the research process.

Process	Plan
Research Question	
Step 1	
Step 2	
Step 3	

Extended Writing Project and Grammar

Skill:
Evaluating Sources

CHECKLIST FOR EVALUATING SOURCES

Once you gather your sources, identify the following:

- where information seems inaccurate, biased, or outdated
- where information strongly relates to your task, purpose, and audience
- where information helps you make an informed decision or solve a problem

In order to conduct advanced searches to gather relevant, credible, and accurate print and digital sources, use the following questions as a guide:

- Is the material published by a well-established source or expert author?
- Is the source material written by a recognized expert on the topic or a well-respected author or organization?
- Is the material up-to-date or based on the most current information?
- Is the source based on factual information that can be verified by another source?
- Is the source material objective and unbiased?
- Does the source contain omissions of important information that supports other viewpoints?
- Does the source contain faulty reasoning?
- Are there discrepancies between the information presented in different sources?

In order to refine your search process, consider the following questions:

- Are there specific terms or phrases that I can use to adjust my search?
- Can I use *and, or,* or *not* to expand or limit my search?
- Can I use quotation marks to search for exact phrases?

Extended Writing Project and Grammar

YOUR TURN

Read the sentences below. Then, complete the chart by sorting the sentences into two categories: those that are credible and reliable and those that are not. Write the corresponding letter for each sentence in the appropriate column.

	Sentences
A	The article states only the author's personal opinions and omits, or leaves out, other positions on the topic.
B	The article includes clear arguments and counterarguments that are supported by factual information.
C	The website is a personal blog or social media website.
D	The author holds a PhD in a discipline related to your topic of research.
E	The text is objective and includes many viewpoints that are properly cited.
F	The text makes unsupported assumptions to persuade readers.

Credible and Reliable	Not Credible or Reliable

Extended Writing Project and Grammar

YOUR TURN

Complete the chart below by filling in the title and author of a source for your informative research essay and answering the questions about this source.

Source Questions	Answers
Source Title and Author:	
Reliability: Has the source material been published in a well-established book or periodical or on a well-established website? Is the source material up-to-date or based on the most current information?	
Accuracy: Is the source based on factual information that can be verified by another source?	
Credibility: Is the source material written by a recognized expert on the topic? Is the source material published by a well-respected author or organization?	
Bias: Is the source material objective and unbiased?	
Omission: Does the source contain omissions of important information that supports other viewpoints?	
Faulty Reasoning: Does the source contain faulty reasoning?	
Decision: Should I use this source in my research essay? Is it effective in answering the research question?	

Reading & Writing Companion

Extended Writing Project and Grammar

Skill:
Research and Notetaking

••• CHECKLIST FOR RESEARCH AND NOTETAKING

In order to conduct short as well as more sustained research projects to answer a question (including a self-generated question) or solve a problem, note the following:

- Answer a question for a research project, or think of your own question that you would like to have answered.
- Look up your topic in an encyclopedia to find general information.
- Find specific, up-to-date information in books and periodicals or on the Internet. If appropriate, conduct interviews with experts to get information.
- Narrow or broaden your inquiry when appropriate.
  > If you find dozens of books on a topic, your research topic may be too broad.
  > If it is difficult to write a research question, narrow your topic so it is more specific.
- Synthesize your information by organizing your notes from various sources to see what the sources have in common and how they differ.

To conduct short as well as more sustained research projects to answer a question (including a self-generated question) or solve a problem, consider the following questions:

- Where could I look to find information?
- How does new information I have found affect my research question?
- How can I demonstrate my understanding of the subject I am investigating?

YOUR TURN

Read each point from a student's note cards below. Then, complete the chart by sorting the points into two categories: those that are relevant and those that are not relevant to the writing topic of recorded music during Ma Rainey's time. Write the corresponding letter for each point in the appropriate column.

	Points
A	Source 1: During the Great Migration, music labels sought to make a profit from the highly popular "race music," which was music recorded by African Americans (Timmel).
B	Source 2: According to *History of Minstrelsy*, the purpose of African-American minstrel shows differed from that of white performers in that "black minstrel performers felt the added responsibility to counter stereotypes of black identity."
C	Source 3: In 1904, Ma Rainey met and married her husband William "Pa" Rainey while performing on tour (Orr).
D	Source 4: The music Rainey recorded with Paramount is of poor quality due to Paramount's "below average recording techniques" (USC Libraries).

Relevant	Not Relevant

Extended Writing Project and Grammar

YOUR TURN

Complete the chart by synthesizing information from sources relevant to your essay subject's work and personal life. Remember to cite and number each source.

Work	Personal Life

Extended Writing Project and Grammar

Research Writing Process: Draft

| PLAN | **DRAFT** | REVISE | EDIT AND PUBLISH |

You have already made progress toward writing your informative research essay. Now it is time to draft your informative research essay.

✏️ WRITE

Use your plan and other responses in your Binder to draft your essay. You may also have new ideas as you begin drafting. Feel free to explore those new ideas as you have them. You can also ask yourself these questions to ensure that your writing is focused, organized, and developed:

Draft Checklist:

☐ **Focused:** Have I made my topic clear to readers? Have I included only relevant information and details and nothing extraneous that might confuse my readers?

☐ **Organized:** Does the organizational structure in my essay make sense? Will readers be engaged by the organization and interested in the way I present information and evidence?

☐ **Developed:** Does my writing include relevant evidence? Will my readers be able to follow my ideas? Will they understand the purpose of my research?

Before you submit your draft, read it over carefully. You want to be sure that you've responded to all aspects of the prompt.

Extended Writing Project and Grammar

Here is Daniela's research essay draft. As you read, notice how Daniela develops her draft to be focused, organized, and developed. As she continues to revise and edit her research essay, she will find and improve weak spots in her writing, as well as correct any language or punctuation mistakes.

NOTES

STUDENT MODEL: FIRST DRAFT

Post-Reconstruction Blues:

How Gertrude "Ma" Rainey Sang Black Rural Southerners into Popular American Culture

Legendary blues vocalist and Harlem Renaissance artist Gertrude "Ma" Rainey, known as the "Mother of Blues," introduced blues music to a mainstream audience, transforming the genre and expanding opportunities for African American artists. Through depictions of black Southern life and the complex experiences of African American women, Rainey's music increased the visibility of a people silenced in popular culture. While less well-known today, Rainey left a legacy that continues to influence and broaden our knowledge of the Post Reconstruction era.

Ella Pridget gave birth to Ma Rainey, originally Gertrude Malissa Nix Pridgett, on April 26, 1886, in Columbus, Georgia. Rainey posessed a musical talent from a young age and performed in public for the first time at age 14 at the Springer Opera House in Columbus. Soon after, she found her calling singing on tour in vaudeville and African American minstral shows. For more than thirty years, performed in troupes, such as F.S. Wolcott's Rabbit Foot Minstrels and Tolliver's Circus and Musical Extravaganza.

~~Ma Rainey used vaudeville and minstrel shows as a platform to showcase her talent. She also used them to share her life experiences. Vaudeville originated from minstrel shows. It became popular at the turn of the century. Vaudeville shows featured unrelated acts such as singing, dancing, comedy, acrobatics, and magic.~~ While no video recordings of Ma Rainey exist, the memory of her vibrint performances have been passed down through written reviews. According to critic Mary L. Bogumil in *Understanding August Wilson*, Rainey wore "flamboyant" jewelry and costmes and performed in front of a

~~backdrop that featured a large gramophone designe, "which gave the appearance of Ma emerging right from the speaker, issuing from and manifesting the music itself" (Timmel). Such extravagant details show the sensational nature of vaudeville shows. Rainey's bold and brilliant stage persona was magnetic she forced the audience, who were often men, to listen to what she had to say.~~

Vaudeville: Ma Rainey's Early Career

Ma Rainey used vaudeville and minstrel shows as a platform to showcase her talent and share her life experiences. Originating from minstrel shows, vaudeville became popular at the turn of the century and featured unrelated acts such as singing, dancing, comedy, acrobatics, and magic. While no video recordings of Ma Rainey exist, the memory of her vibrant performances has been passed down through written reviews. According to critic Mary L. Bogumil in *Understanding August Wilson*, Rainey wore "flamboyant" jewelry and costumes and performed in front of a backdrop that featured a large gramophone design, "which gave the appearance of Ma emerging right from the speaker, issuing from and manifesting the music itself" (qtd. in Timmel). Such extravagant details exemplify the sensational nature of vaudeville shows. Rainey's bold and brilliant stage persona was magnetic. She forced the audience, who were often men, to listen to what she had to say.

~~The variety show format of vaudeville allowed performers to communicate larger themes to the audience. For example, PBS's *American Masters* says of immigrant performers, "Their acts were a form of assimilation, in which they could become active parts of popular culture through representations of their heritage" ("Vaudeville: About Vaudeville"). However, as an African American woman, she belonged to a class of citizens who were underrepresented, misunderstood, and discriminated against. Ma Rainey was not an immigrant. Like the immigrants, she used the modes of performance available to her to cross racial and class boundaries and bring the experiences of a Southern African American women into the main stream ("Vaudeville: About Vaudeville").~~

Skill: Print and Graphic Features

Daniela decides that she could make her points clearer by using headings, so she inserts a heading between her second and third paragraphs. As she continues to reread her essay, she will add a heading wherever she discusses a new aspect of Ma Rainey's work and life.

NOTES

 Skill: Paraphrasing

Daniela realizes she has taken the phrase "to cross racial and class boundaries" word-for-word from her source. To avoid plagiarism, she can either paraphrase the information or quote it. Since she already has one quotation from this source in the paragraph, she decides to paraphrase.

Skill: Critiquing Research

Instead of synthesizing information from several sources, Daniela has used only one source in the paragraph. To round out her explanation of Vaudeville and Ma Rainey's role in it, she integrates another idea from a different source into the paragraph.

The variety show format of vaudeville allowed performers to communicate larger themes to the audience. For example, PBS's *American Masters* says of immigrant performers, "Their acts were a form of assimilation, in which they could become active parts of popular culture through representations of their heritage" ("Vaudeville: About Vaudeville"). In other words, immigrant performers used the highly adaptable and entertaining structure of vaudeville to disseminate information about where they came from. Ma Rainey was not an immigrant. However, as an African-American woman, she belonged to a class of citizens who were underrepresented, misunderstood, and discriminated against. Like the immigrants, she used the modes of performance available to her to subvert boundaries and bring the experiences of Southern African-American women into the mainstream ("Vaudeville: About Vaudeville"). That Ma Rainey was also the first woman to include blues music in her act only further illustrates her ability to use this mode of performance to break barriers and convey an important message (Orr).

The blues played a central part in Rainey's performances. Originating in the South at the turn of the century, blues came from such African musical traditions as field hollers, work songs, spirituals, and country string ballads ("What Is the Blues?"). Most blues songs follow a 12 bar structure with an AAB verse pattern where "the first and second lines are repeated, and the third line is a response to them—often with a twist" ("Understanding the 12-Bar Blues"). Blues music tends to explore melancholy topics, such as sadness, desire, and longing. Many of Rainey's songs had a melancholy tone, her music served to empower women by approaching topics most women could not discuss freely. For example, Ma Rainey's candid discussion of love was unique to blues artists of her time. She was lonely but also embraced her independence ("I don't want no man to put sugar in my tea."). Rainey's rejection of a male partner was radical because women in this time period were expected to build their lives around being married and building a family. In *Blues Legacies and Black Feminism*, Angela Davis points out that "black women of that era were acknowledging and addressing issues central to contemporary feminist discourse" (Davis 28). Black female blues artists like Ma

Extended Writing Project and Grammar

Rainey were ahead of their time in terms of asserting their agency. Rainey's performance of this song introduced the idea of liberated black women into the mainstream.

~~Rainey's vocals had a deep and unbellished tone expressing raw emotion that resonated with a wide range of audiences. The gravelly timbre of her . . . raspy, deep voice (Orr) as well as her "moaning style" entranced listeners. Her flashy visual representation attracted the attention of the audience. Her measured and gripping delivery kept them waiting for more. Ma Rainey one of the first professional female blues artists to make a phonograph record. During the Great Migration, blues music spread from the South into other regions of the nation. By the 1920s, recording labels saw a market for "race records," or music created by and for African Americans. After establishing her career as a touring musician, Ma Rainey recorded over 100 songs with Paramount in the span of 1923 to 1928. One could argue that Paramount exploited Ma Rainey for corporate gane. However, in 1928 Paramount stopped recording with Rainey after determining that race records like hers were no longer profitable. Still, making a phonograph record with Paramount did help Rainey's audience and success grow. Over the course of her career, she performed alongside various bands and other renowned Harlem Renaissance muzicians, such as Louis Armstrong and Bessie Smith.~~

Rainey's vocals had a deep and unembellished tone expressing raw emotion that resonated with a wide range of audiences. "The gravelly timbre of her . . . raspy, deep voice" (Orr) as well as her "moaning style" (Timmel) entranced listeners. Her flashy visual representation attracted the attention of the audience. Her measured and gripping delivery kept them waiting for more. Ma Rainey was one of the first professional female blues artists to make a phonograph record. During the Great Migration, blues music spread from the South into other regions of the nation. [Include graphic] By the 1920s, recording labels saw a market for "race records," or music created by and for African Americans. After establishing her career as a touring musician, Ma Rainey

Skill: Sources and Citations

Daniela forgot to add quotation marks around the description from N. Lee Orr, so she adds them. In the same sentence, she forgot to add a parenthetical citation for the quotation "moaning style." She includes the author's name in the citation, but since the source is electronic, she doesn't add a page number.

recorded over 100 songs with Paramount in the span of 1923 to 1928 (Timmel). However, in 1928 Paramount stopped recording with Rainey after determining that race records like hers were no longer profitable. One could argue that Paramount exploited Ma Rainey for corporate gain. Still, making a phonograph record with Paramount did help Rainey's audience and success grow. Over the course of her career, she performed alongside various bands and other renowned Harlem Renaissance musicians, such as Louis Armstrong and Bessie Smith.

In an era when women of color had limited possibilities, "The Mother of Blues," Ma Rainey, was a musician who took advantage of the modes of performance that were available to her to build a long lasting career. Rainey used the public platforms of vaudeville and recorded music. Her lyrics talked about her experiences and feelings. Ma Rainey's unique style appealed to many people, helping bring the blues and her life experiences to a mainstream audience.

Works Cited

Biography.com Editors. "Ma Rainey Biography." *The Biography.com Website,* A&E Television Networks, Published 2 Apr. 2014, Updated 27 Apr. 2017, https://www.biography.com/people/ma-rainey-9542413. Accessed 20 Sep. 2018.

Davis, Angela Y. Blues Legacies and Black Feminism: Gertrude "Ma" Rainey, Bessie Smith, and Billie Holiday. *Google Books.* 2nd ed., Vintage Books, 1999.

Orr, N. Lee. "Gertrude 'Ma' Rainey (1886-1939)." *New Georgia Encyclopedia,* Georgia State University, 9 May 2003, https://www.georgiaencyclopedia.org/articles/arts-culture/gertrude-ma-rainey-1886-1939. Accessed 20 Sep. 2018.

Timmel, Lisa. "The Music of Ma Rainey." *Huntington Theater Company,* Accessed 20 Sep. 2018.

"Understanding the 12-Bar Blues." *PBS: The Blues*, 2003, www.pbs.org/theblues/classroom/essays12bar.html. Accessed 21 Sep. 2018.

"Vaudeville: About Vaudeville." *PBS: American Masters*, 8 Oct. 1999, www.pbs.org/wnet/americanmasters/vaudeville-about-vaudeville/721/. Accessed 20 Sep. 2018.

"What Is the Blues?" *PBS: The Blues*, 2003, www.pbs.org/theblues/classroom/essaysblues.html. Accessed 21 Sep. 2018.

Skill: Critiquing Research

••• CHECKLIST FOR CRITIQUING RESEARCH

In order to conduct short or sustained research projects to answer a question or solve a problem, drawing on several sources, do the following:

- narrow or broaden the question or inquiry as necessary when researching your topic

- use advanced search terms effectively when looking for information online, such as using unique terms that are specific to your topic (i.e., "daily life in Jamestown, Virginia" rather than just "Jamestown, Virginia")

- assess the strengths and limitations of each source in terms of the task, purpose, and audience

- synthesize and integrate multiple sources on a subject

To evaluate and use relevant information while conducting short or sustained research projects, consider the following questions:

- Did I narrow or broaden my research inquiry as needed?

- Are there specific terms or phrases in my research question that I can use to adjust my search?

- Can I use *and, or,* or *not* to expand or limit my search?

- Can I use quotation marks to search for exact phrases?

- Have I successfully synthesized and integrated multiple sources on my topic?

Extended Writing Project and Grammar

 YOUR TURN

Read the previous draft of Daniela's research plan below, and then choose the best answer to each question about it.

> Major Research Question: Did Ma Rainey influence other musicians?
>
> List of Sources:
> 1. Facebook Post: Bessie Smith v. Ma Rainey
> 2. The Legacy of Blues Musicians: Mamie Smith, Ma Rainey, and Beyond (television documentary)
> 3. Britannica.com: Ma Rainey's Blues Style
> 4. Classic Blues Magazine: Classic Blues Traditions, Then and Now

1. Which revision of her major research question will best refocus her research plan?
   - A. What are the topics of Ma Rainey's lyrics?
   - B. How did Ma Rainey's blues style influence other musicians?
   - C. Why was Bessie Smith a successful blues singer?
   - D. The research question is already focused.

2. Which source should Daniela consider replacing?
   - A. 1
   - B. 2
   - C. 3
   - D. 4

 WRITE

Write your major research question, and list your sources. Then, use the questions in the checklist to critique your research plan. In your critique, evaluate the appropriateness of your sources and determine whether your research plan needs a revision.

Extended Writing Project and Grammar

Skill:
Paraphrasing

••• CHECKLIST FOR PARAPHRASING

In order to integrate information into your research essay, first make sure you understand what the author is saying after reading the text carefully. Then, note the following:

- any words or expressions in the text that are unfamiliar

- words and phrases that are important to include in a paraphrase to maintain the meaning of the text

- potential instances of plagiarism in your essay; avoid plagiarism by acknowledging all sources for both paraphrased and quoted material, and avoid overly relying on any one source

- whether or not your integration of information maintains a logical flow of ideas

To integrate information into your research essay, consider the following questions:

- Do I understand the meaning of the text? Have I determined the meanings of any words in the text that are unfamiliar to me?

- Does my paraphrase of the text maintain the text's original meaning? Have I missed any key points or details?

- Have I avoided plagiarism by acknowledging all my sources for both paraphrased and quoted material and avoided overly relying on any one source?

- Did I integrate information selectively to maintain a logical flow of ideas?

Extended Writing Project and Grammar

 YOUR TURN

Choose the best answer to each question.

1. The following is a quotation that Daniela is considering including in her essay. Which of the following sentences provides the best paraphrase of the source text?

> "Today, the blues no longer commands the attention it once did; to many young listeners, traditional blues—if not contemporary blues—may sound antiquated and uninteresting."

○ A. Once a very popular genre, blues music is not as widely enjoyed by today's young listeners.
○ B. Many young listeners are unfamiliar with the blues today.
○ C. The history of traditional blues spans several generations.
○ D. Today, the blues no longer commands the attention it once did.

2. The following is a paragraph from a previous draft of Daniela's essay. How could paraphrasing best help Daniela improve this paragraph?

> Rainey's vocals had a deep and unembellished tone expressing raw emotion that resonated with a wide range of audiences. "The gravelly timbre of her... raspy, deep voice" (Orr) as well as her "moaning style" (Timmel) entranced listeners. "Her material consisted of a variety of songs drawn from Southern traditions" (Timmel) and her flashy visual representation attracted the attention of the audience. Her measured and gripping delivery kept them waiting for more. Ma Rainey was one of the first professional female blues artists to make a phonograph record. During the Great Migration, blues music spread from the South into other regions of the nation. By the 1920s, recording labels saw a market for "race records," (Timmel) or music created by and for African Americans. After establishing her career as a touring musician, Ma Rainey "laid down over 100 tracks between 1923 and 1928" (Timmel).

○ A. Paraphrasing would help improve this paragraph by showing that Daniela thoroughly read each of her sources.
○ B. Paraphrasing would improve her paragraph by making it shorter and quicker to read.
○ C. Paraphrasing would increase Daniela's chances of plagiarizing information.
○ D. Paraphrasing would help improve her paragraph by avoiding so many back-to-back quotations and maintaining a logical flow of ideas.

 WRITE

Use the questions in the checklist to paraphrase information from a source and integrate it into a paragraph of your informative research essay.

Extended Writing Project and Grammar

Skill:
Sources and Citations

••• CHECKLIST FOR SOURCES AND CITATIONS

In order to gather relevant information from multiple authoritative print and digital sources and to cite the sources correctly, do the following:

- gather information from a variety of print and digital sources, using search terms to effectively narrow your search
- assess the strengths and limitations of each source in regard to your task, your purpose for writing, and your audience
  > find information on authors to see if they are experts on a topic
  > look at the publication date to see if the information is current
- avoid relying on any one source, and synthesize information from a variety of books, publications, and online resources
- quote or paraphrase the information you find, and cite it to avoid plagiarism
- integrate information selectively to maintain a logical flow of ideas in your essay, using transitional words and phrases
- include all sources in a bibliography, following a standard format:
  > Halall, Ahmed. *The Pyramids of Ancient Egypt*. New York: Central Publishing, 2016.
  > for a citation, footnote, or endnote, include the author, title, and page number

To check that you have gathered information and cited sources correctly, consider the following questions:

- Have I assessed the strengths and limitations of each source?
- Have I looked for different points of view, instead of relying on one source?
- Did I cite the information I found using a standard format to avoid plagiarism?
- Did I include all my sources in my bibliography?

YOUR TURN

Choose the best answer to each question.

1. Below is a section from a previous draft of Daniela's research paper. What change should Daniela make to improve the clarity of her citation?

   > Author Sandra R. Lieb writes, "The Classic Blues barely outlived the twenties, becoming engulfed in and utterly changed by the Depression and shifts in audience taste, but from 1920 to roughly 1928 Ma Rainey and [other women singers] were the greatest artists, enjoying a period of influence, wealth, popularity, and imitation by lesser performers."

   - A. Add the page number in parentheses after the quotation.
   - B. Add the author's last name in parentheses after the quotation.
   - C. Add the author's last name and page number in parentheses after the quotation.
   - D. No change needs to be made.

2. Below is a section from a previous draft of Daniela's works cited page in the MLA format. Which revision best corrects her style errors?

   > *Mother of Blues: A Study of Ma Rainey.* by Sandra R. Lieb. University of Massachusetts Press, 1981.

   - A. Lieb, Sandra R. Mother of Blues: A Study of Ma Rainey. University of Massachusetts Press, 1981.
   - B. University of Massachusetts Press, 1981. Lieb, Sandra R. *Mother of Blues: A Study of Ma Rainey.*
   - C. Lieb, Sandra R. *Mother of Blues: A Study of Ma Rainey.* University of Massachusetts Press.
   - D. Lieb, Sandra R. *Mother of Blues: A Study of Ma Rainey.* University of Massachusetts Press, 1981.

WRITE

Use the questions in the checklist to revise your in-text citations and works cited list.

Extended Writing Project and Grammar

Skill:
Print and Graphic Features

••• CHECKLIST FOR PRINT AND GRAPHIC FEATURES

In order to check your draft for the inclusion of print and graphic features, first reread your draft and ask yourself the following questions:

- To what extent would including formatting, graphics, or multimedia be effective in achieving my purpose?
- Which formatting, graphics, or multimedia seem most important in conveying information to the reader?
- How is the addition of the formatting, graphics, or multimedia useful in aiding comprehension?

To include formatting, graphics, and multimedia, use the following questions as a guide:

- How can I use formatting to better organize information? Consider adding:
  > titles
  > headings
  > subheadings
  > bullets
  > boldface and italicized terms

- How can I use graphics to better convey information? Consider adding:
  > charts
  > graphs
  > tables
  > timelines
  > diagrams
  > maps
  > figures and statistics

- How can I use multimedia to add interest and variety? Consider adding a combination of:
  > photographs
  > art
  > audio
  > video

164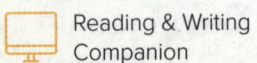

Please note that excerpts and passages in the StudySync® library and this workbook are intended as touchstones to generate interest in an author's work. The excerpts and passages do not substitute for the reading of entire texts, and StudySync® strongly recommends that students seek out and purchase the whole literary or informational work in order to experience it as the author intended. Links to online resellers are available in our digital library. In addition, complete works may be ordered through an authorized reseller by filling out and returning to StudySync® the order form enclosed in this workbook.

YOUR TURN

Choose the best answer to each question.

1. Read the following two paragraphs from another draft of Daniela's essay. Then, decide which of the possible headings below she should insert between the paragraphs to best improve the flow of information between them.

> The variety show format of vaudeville allowed performers to communicate larger themes to the audience. For example, PBS's *American Masters* says of immigrant performers, "Their acts were a form of assimilation, in which they could become active parts of popular culture through representations of their heritage" ("Vaudeville: About Vaudeville"). In other words, immigrant performers used the highly adaptable and entertaining structure of vaudeville to disseminate information about where they came from. Ma Rainey was not an immigrant. However, as an African-American woman, she belonged to a class of citizens who were underrepresented, misunderstood, and discriminated against. Like the immigrants, she used the modes of performance available to her "to cross racial and class boundaries" ("Vaudeville: About Vaudeville") and bring the experiences of a Southern African-American women into the mainstream.
>
> The blues played a central part in Rainey's performances. Originating in the South at the turn of the century, blues emerged from such African musical traditions as field hollers, work songs, spirituals, and country string ballads ("What Is the Blues?"). Most blues songs follow a 12-bar structure with an AAB verse pattern where "the first and second lines are repeated, and the third line is a response to them—often with a twist" ("Understanding the 12-Bar Blues"). Blues music tends to explore melancholy topics, such as sadness, desire, and longing. While many of Rainey's songs had a melancholy tone, her music also served to empower women by approaching topics most women could not discuss freely.

- A. "Moving On from Vaudeville"
- B. "Ma Rainey and Her Influence on the Blues"
- C. "The Blues"
- D. Daniela does not need to include a heading between these two paragraphs.

WRITE

Use the questions in the checklist to review your essay and locate where you can place headings to call out specific sections and topics. Then, note places where you would like to add graphics or media, and describe what sort of features you might include and why.

Extended Writing Project and Grammar

Research Writing Process: Revise

| PLAN | DRAFT | **REVISE** | EDIT AND PUBLISH |

You have written a draft of your informative research essay. You have also received input from your peers about how to improve it. Now you are going to revise your draft.

⮜ REVISION GUIDE

Examine your draft to find areas for revision. Use the guide below to help you review:

Review	Revise	Example
Clarity		
Highlight a sentence that shows your purpose for writing.	Make sure the purpose is specific and clearly stated for your audience.	While less well-known today, Rainey left a legacy that continues to influence musicians and broaden our knowledge of life for African Americans in the Post Reconstruction era.
Development		
Identify the textual evidence you quote in support of your thesis.	Rather than letting quotations speak for themselves, make sure you provide original commentary to build upon your evidence from sources.	For example, PBS's *American Masters* says of immigrant performers, "Their acts were a form of assimilation, in which they could become active parts of popular culture through representations of their heritage" ("Vaudeville: About Vaudeville"). In other words, immigrant performers used the highly adaptable and entertaining structure of vaudeville to disseminate information about where they came from.

Extended Writing Project and Grammar

Review	Revise	Example
Organization		
Review your body paragraphs. Are they focused and logically organized? Identify and annotate any sentences within and across paragraphs that don't flow in a clear and logical way.	Rewrite the sentences so they appear in a clear and logical order.	~~One could argue that Paramount exploited Ma Rainey for corporate gane.~~ However, in 1928 Paramount stopped recording with Rainey after determining that race records like hers were no longer profitable. One could argue that Paramount exploited Ma Rainey for corporate gane. Still, making a phonograph record with Paramount did help Rainey's audience and success grow.
Style: Word Choice		
Identify any weak adjectives or verbs.	Replace weak adjectives and verbs with strong, descriptive adjectives and verbs.	Such extravagant details ~~show~~ exemplify the sensational nature of vaudeville shows.
Style: Sentence Fluency		
Read aloud your writing and listen to the way the text sounds. Does it sound choppy? Or does it flow smoothly with rhythm, movement, and emphasis on important details and events?	Rewrite a key passage, making your sentences longer or shorter to achieve a better flow of writing.	Ma Rainey used vaudeville and minstrel shows as a platform to showcase her talent. ~~She also used them to~~ and share her life experiences. ~~Vaudeville originated~~ Originating from minstrel shows~~.~~, ~~It~~ vaudeville became popular at the turn of the century~~.~~ ~~Vaudeville shows~~ and featured unrelated acts such as singing, dancing, comedy, acrobatics, and magic.

✏️ WRITE

Use the revision guide, as well as your peer reviews, to help you evaluate your informative research essay to determine places that should be revised.

Extended Writing Project and Grammar

Skill:
Using a Style Guide

••• CHECKLIST FOR USING A STYLE GUIDE

In order to write your work so that it conforms to the guidelines in a style manual, do the following:

- Determine which style guide you should use before you write your draft.
  > Follow the guidelines chosen by a teacher, for example.
  > Familiarize yourself with that guide, and check your writing against the guide when you edit.

- Use the style guide for the overall formatting of your paper, citation style, bibliography format, and other style considerations for reporting research.

As you draft, use an additional style guide, such as *Artful Sentences: Syntax as Style* by Virginia Tufte, to help you vary your syntax, or the grammatical structure of sentences.

  > Use a variety of simple, compound, complex, and compound-complex sentences to convey information.
  > Be sure to punctuate your sentences correctly.
  > Follow standard English language conventions to help you maintain a formal style for formal papers.

To edit your work so that it conforms to the guidelines in a style manual, consider the following questions:

- Have I followed the conventions for spelling, punctuation, capitalization, sentence structure, and formatting, according to the style guide?
- Have I varied my syntax to make my information clear for readers?
- Do I have an entry in my works cited or bibliography for each reference I used?
- Have I followed the correct style, including the guidelines for capitalization and punctuation, in each entry in my works cited or bibliography?

Extended Writing Project and Grammar

YOUR TURN

Read the types of information below. Then, complete the chart by sorting them into two categories: those that are found in a style guide and those that are not. Write the corresponding letter for each type of information in the appropriate column.

Types of Information	
A. proper punctuation for quotations	F. a list of possible research topics
B. synonyms for a word	G. how to format a bibliography
C. how to read a map	H. how to cite internet sources
D. when to use a hyphen	I. the definition of a word
E. how to write an outline	J. when to use italics

In a Style Guide	Not in a Style Guide

WRITE

Use the checklist to help you choose a convention that you have found challenging to follow. Use a credible style guide to check and correct any errors related to that convention in your research essay.

Extended Writing Project and Grammar

Grammar: Contested Usage

For most formal writing, it is probably advisable to follow the traditional rules of grammar. In most cases, following the rules will improve both the clarity and effectiveness of your communication. However, there are a number of grammar "rules" that can be broken if you have a good reason to do so. The most important thing to keep in mind is that no rule of grammar should be broken unless it is done deliberately to improve the effectiveness of your writing.

The series comma is still widely used and preferred for a series of three or more items. However, in recent years, its necessity has come into question. Many authors of formal and informal writing find that they can use other strategies that eliminate the need for the series comma.

Strategy	Text
Sometimes you can omit a series comma if the wording clearly indicates a new phrase in the series.	Paul **writes** novels, **paints** pottery and **designs** gardens.
Sometimes you can omit a series comma if single words are clearly related to one reference or topic.	In an attempt to get to the bottom of the question once and for all, the *Guardian* has gathered writers from the fields of **science, psychotherapy, literature, religion and philosophy** to give their definition of the much-pondered word. What is Love?

The words *whom* and *who* are a great example of contested diction. *Who* is a subject pronoun, like *he, she,* or *they*. It is used as a subject in a main clause that asks a question or as the subject in a subordinate clause. *Whom* is an object pronoun, like *him, her,* or *them*. It is used in place of *who* as the direct object that receives the action of a verb or as the object of a preposition. If you are writing for an informational or research purpose, use *whom* when referring to a pronoun as an object. However, if you are writing informally, with contemporary dialogue, colloquialisms, or slang, it is appropriate to eliminate the use of *whom*.

Occasionally, writers choose to begin sentences with coordinating conjunctions. Writers use coordinating conjunctions as sentence openers when they want to indicate a relationship with the previous sentence, but do not want to combine the two complete thoughts into one sentence. This is usually done to emphasize the second of two related ideas.

Extended Writing Project and Grammar

Strategy	Text
If you are writing two or three sentences that are closely related and have equal importance, you could use a coordinating conjunction such as *and* or *but* as a sentence opener.	So when Miss Lawington told me about the cakes I thought that I could bake them and earn enough at one time to increase the net value of the flock the equivalent of two head. **And** that by saving the eggs out one at a time, even the eggs wouldn't be costing anything. As I Lay Dying

🔄 YOUR TURN

1. When can a series comma be omitted?

   ○ A. A series comma must always be used, even if the items are clearly related to one reference or topic.

   ○ B. A series comma can be omitted if single items are clearly related to one reference or topic.

2. Is the removal of the series comma in this sentence acceptable?

   > Would you like your eggs scrambled, fried or poached?

   ○ A. Yes, removing the series comma is acceptable.

   ○ B. No, removing the series comma is unacceptable.

3. Is this use of a coordinating conjunction as a sentence opener acceptable?

   > He spent his vacation in Naples, Florida. But he said it was a business, not a pleasure, trip.

   ○ A. Yes, it is an acceptable use of a coordinating conjunction as a sentence opener.

   ○ B. No, it is an unacceptable use of a coordinating conjunction as a sentence opener.

4. Is this an acceptable use of *who*?

   > In 1864, Twain, who fortune still eluded, went to San Francisco where he worked on several newspapers.

   ○ A. Yes, it is an acceptable use of *who*.

   ○ B. No, it is an unacceptable use of *who*. It should be replaced with *whom*.

Extended Writing Project and Grammar

Grammar: Hyphens

Hyphens join words or parts of words. Do not use any type of dash where a hyphen is needed.

Rule	Text	Explanation
Use a hyphen after any prefix joined to a proper noun or a proper adjective, for example, *pre-Depression*. Use a hyphen after the prefixes *all-*, *ex-* (meaning "former"), and *self-* joined to any noun or adjective. Use a hyphen after the prefix *anti-* when it is joined to a word beginning with *i*. Also, use a hyphen after the prefix *vice-*, except in *vice president*.	After Reconstruction, the new South was in some ways similar to the **pre-Civil War** South: White Southern Democrats returned to power, and African Americans lost many of their civil rights. American Literature & History: The Civil War Era (1850-1880)	The prefix **pre-** is joined to the proper noun **Civil War** with a hyphen.
Hyphenate any compound word that is a spelled-out cardinal number (such as *twenty-one*) or ordinal number (such as *twenty-first*) up to *ninety-nine* or *ninety-ninth*. Hyphenate any spelled-out fraction.	**One-eighth** of the whole population were . . . slaves, not distributed generally over the Union, but localized in the southern part of it. Lincoln's Second Inaugural Address	**One-eighth** is a fraction.
Use a hyphen in a compound adjective that precedes a noun. Be sure to choose words carefully as the words should work together to provide a unified meaning.	It might be, too, that a witch, like old Mistress Hibbins, the **bitter-tempered** widow of the magistrate, was to die upon the gallows. The Scarlet Letter	The words **bitter-tempered** are hyphenated as a compound adjective that modifies the noun *widow*.

Extended Writing Project and Grammar

YOUR TURN

1. How should this sentence be changed?

   > Sandra Wilson—the exmayor of our fair city—spoke warmly of the new, experienced mayor.

   - A. Change **exmayor** to **ex-mayor.**
   - B. Change the dashes to hyphens.
   - C. Change **new, experienced** to **new-experienced.**
   - D. No change needs to be made to this sentence.

2. How should this sentence be changed?

   > The short-tempered coach made the team do twenty five extra sit-ups before the end of practice—how unfair!

   - A. Remove the hyphen in **short-tempered.**
   - B. Change **twenty five** to **twenty-five.**
   - C. Change the dash to a hyphen.
   - D. No change needs to be made to this sentence.

3. How should this sentence be changed?

   > My grandfather—a two-tour veteran—loves telling stories about how newfound optimism spread through post-World War II America.

   - A. Change the dashes to hyphens.
   - B. Change **newfound** to **new-found.**
   - C. Change **post-World War II** to **post World War II.**
   - D. No change needs to be made to this sentence.

Extended Writing Project and Grammar

Research Writing Process: Edit and Publish

| PLAN | DRAFT | REVISE | **EDIT AND PUBLISH** |

You have revised your informative research essay based on your peer feedback and your own examination.

Now, it is time to edit your essay. When you revised, you focused on the content of your essay. You probably critiqued your research and made sure you paraphrased sources correctly and avoided plagiarism. When you edit, you focus on the mechanics of your writing, paying close attention to things like grammar and punctuation.

Use the checklist below to guide you as you edit:

☐ Have I followed all the rules for hyphens?

☐ Have I checked for contested usage and selected the usage that is most appropriate for my purpose?

☐ Do I have any sentence fragments or run-on sentences?

☐ Have I spelled everything correctly?

Notice some edits Daniela has made:

- Used the passive voice to remove less important information
- Corrected spelling errors
- Hyphenated a compound adjective preceding a noun
- Added a subject to correct a sentence fragment

> ~~Ella Pridget gave birth to Ma Rainey, originally~~ Ma Rainey was born Gertrude Malissa Nix Pridgett~~,~~ on April 26, 1886, in Columbus, Georgia. Rainey ~~posessed~~ possessed a musical talent from a young age and performed in public for the first time at age 14 at the Springer Opera House in Columbus. Soon after, she found her calling singing on tour in vaudeville and African-American ~~minstral~~ minstrel shows. For more than thirty years, Rainey performed in troupes, such as F.S. Wolcott's Rabbit Foot Minstrels and Tolliver's Circus and Musical Extravaganza.

WRITE

Use the questions in the checklist, as well as your peer reviews, to help you evaluate your informative research essay to determine areas that need editing. Then, edit your essay to correct those errors.

Once you have made all your corrections, you are ready to publish your work. You can distribute your writing to family and friends, hang it on a bulletin board, or post it on your blog. If you publish online, share the link with your family, friends, and classmates.

Fighting for Justice

INFORMATIONAL TEXT

Introduction

In a court of law, decisions are made that can affect an entire society. However, these decisions are not always fair or just. The Hansberry family recognized discriminatory laws in the 1940s and didn't give up until the court changed its mind. This family's court case, Hansberry v. Lee, helped correct an injustice in the legal system and inspired a famous play, *A Raisin in the Sun*.

Fighting for Justice

VOCABULARY

legal
based on the law or required by law

valid
acceptable, reasonable or legally official

outcome
the way something turns out

previous
existing before something else

READ

Fighting for Justice

1. Imagine moving into the house of your dreams. You love the neighborhood. You're excited to unpack your things and call a new place home. Then, your new neighbors decide that you can't live in that neighborhood because of the color of your skin. They tell your family to leave the new house. They have **legal** documents from the court to force you to do so.

2. Believe it or not, this terrible situation actually happened to African American families. Even though forcing someone out of a neighborhood based on race is one of the most awful actions, one family made this negative event have a better **outcome**. The Hansberry family forever changed the law.

Standing up for justice

3. In 1940, Mr. Carl Augustus Hansberry and his family bought a house in Woodlawn, Illinois. The Hansberrys were excited to move in. However, soon after they bought their new house, they heard from their neighbors, the Lee family. The Lees told the Hansberrys that they couldn't live in the neighborhood because they were African American. Mr. Lee told Mr. Hansberry that the other homeowners in the neighborhood had signed a restrictive covenant. This particular legal document said that African Americans couldn't live there.

Fighting for Justice

NOTES

4   The Hansberrys knew that the restrictive covenant was unfair. They also said that the document was not **valid** because not all of the neighbors had signed it. The Hansberrys decided to fight in court for their right to live in their house. Their case would later become one of the most famous cases to ever exist: Hansberry v. Lee.

5   The members of the Hansberry family were the defendants. Defendants are people who are accused of doing something wrong. The Lee family and other neighbors said that the Hansberrys had no chance of winning the case. They said the court had already decided in 1934 that denying African Americans the right to live in a neighborhood was allowed. This case was called Burke v. Kleiman.

6   In fact, the Lees did win. The law stated that since the court already made a decision in the case of Burke v. Kleiman, no one else could fight a similar case and win. However, the Hansberrys knew that this was unjust. They weren't going to give up. They decided to take their case to the Supreme Court of the United States in Washington, D.C.

All the way to the Supreme Court

7   Using the legal system is the correct way to fight injustice. For the Hansberry family, it was also dangerous. Years later, Mr. Hansberry's daughter, Lorraine, recalled being treated in the worst way. She wrote, "My memories of this 'correct' way of fighting white supremacy in America include being spat at, cursed and pummeled in the daily trek to and from school."

8   Lorraine's mother had to protect the family while her father was in Washington, D.C. Lorraine wrote, "And I also remember my desperate and courageous mother, patrolling our household all night."

Justice finally wins

9   In the end the Supreme Court agreed with the Hansberrys that a restrictive covenant could not be legal if only about half of the neighbors had signed it. In addition, they reversed the law that said the Hansberrys couldn't fight the case because of the court's **previous** decision in 1934 in the case of Burke v. Kleiman. This ruling made court cases fairer for everyone.

10 Today, the Hansberrys are famous for another reason as well. Lorraine Hansberry became a famous and respected playwright. She wrote *A Raisin in the Sun*. The play is based on her family's fight for justice and the right to live where they wanted.

11. The court exists so that people can have the chance to fight for what's fair. The Hansberry family helped us all to achieve this goal. Thanks to the Hansberry family, fighting for justice became much easier for all of us.

THE AMERICAN COURT SYSTEM

THE COURT'S ROLES
- enforce certain laws
- interpret laws
- overturn unconstitutional laws
- make certain types of new laws

THE TYPES OF COURTS
- Trial — first courts to hear and rule on cases
- Appellate — higher courts that review decisions from trial courts. The U.S. Supreme Court is an example of an appellate court.

THE TYPES OF CASES
- Criminal — prosecutes a defendant for violation of the government's criminal laws
- Civil — resolves a legal dispute over rights established by the Constitution or under federal or state law

Fighting for Justice

First Read

Read "Fighting for Justice." After you read, complete the Think Questions below.

THINK QUESTIONS

1. Why do some people not want the Hansberrys living in their neighborhood?

   Some people do not want the Hansberrys living in their neighborhood because _____.

2. How do the Hansberrys fight for the right to live in the neighborhood?

   The Hansberrys _____.

3. At the end of the text, how do the Hansberrys win their fight for justice? Include evidence from the text to support your response.

   The Hansberrys win by _____.

4. Use context to confirm the meaning of the word *legal* as it is used in "Fighting for Justice." Write your definition of *legal* here.

   Legal means _____.

   A context clue is _____.

5. What is another way to say the Hansberrys were happy with the *outcome* of the trial?

   The Hansberrys were happy _____.

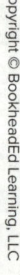

Fighting for Justice

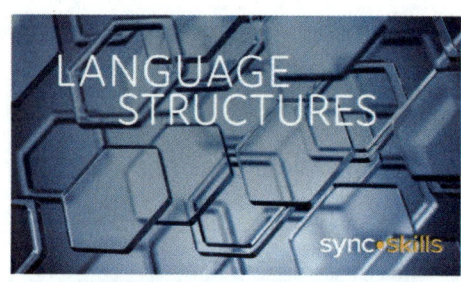

Skill:
Language Structures

★ DEFINE

In every language, there are rules that tell how to **structure** sentences. These rules define the correct order of words. In the English language, for example, a **basic** structure for sentences is subject, verb, and object. Some sentences have more **complicated** structures.

You will encounter both basic and complicated **language structures** in the classroom materials you read. Being familiar with language structures will help you better understand the text.

••• CHECKLIST FOR LANGUAGE STRUCTURES

To improve your comprehension of language structures, do the following:

- ✓ Monitor your understanding.
    - Ask yourself: Why do I not understand this sentence? Is it because I do not understand some of the words? Or is it because I do not understand the way the words are ordered in the sentence?
- ✓ Break down the sentence into its parts.
    - Pay attention to comparatives and superlatives. The **comparative** form compares two things. The **superlative** form compares more than two things.
    - Ask yourself: Are there comparatives or superlatives in this sentence? What are they comparing?
- ✓ Confirm your understanding with a peer or teacher.

Fighting for Justice

YOUR TURN

Complete the chart by writing each word in the correct "Comparative" and "Superlative" columns.

Word Options				
best	more creative	better	fastest	hardest
harder	faster	happiest	most creative	happier

Adjective	Comparative	Superlative
fast		
hard		
happy		
good		
creative		

Fighting for Justice

Skill: Visual and Contextual Support

★ DEFINE

Visual support is an image or an object that helps you understand a text. **Contextual support** is a **feature** that helps you understand a text. By using visual and contextual supports, you can develop your vocabulary so you can better understand a variety of texts.

First, preview the text to identify any visual supports. These might include illustrations, graphics, charts, or other objects in a text. Then, identify any contextual supports. Examples of contextual supports are titles, headers, captions, and boldface terms. Write down your **observations**.

Then, write down what those visual and contextual supports tell you about the meaning of the text. Note any new vocabulary that you see in those supports. Ask your peers and your teacher to **confirm** your understanding of the text.

••• CHECKLIST FOR VISUAL AND CONTEXTUAL SUPPORT

To use visual and contextual support to understand texts, do the following:

- ✓ Preview the text. Read the title, headers, and other features. Look at any images and graphics.
- ✓ Write down the visual and contextual supports in the text.
- ✓ Write down what those supports tell you about the text.
- ✓ Note any new vocabulary that you see in those supports.
- ✓ Create an illustration for the reading and write a descriptive caption.
- ✓ Confirm your observations with your peers and teacher.

Fighting for Justice

YOUR TURN

Read each of the phrases below. Then, complete the chart by sorting the phrases into those that provide visual support and those that provide contextual support.

	Options
A	an illustration of the human body
B	a graphic that shows the American system of checks and balances
C	a boldface vocabulary word
D	the title of a biography about a famous painter
E	a caption that explains a photograph
F	a chart comparing the three branches of government
G	headers dividing an article into sections
H	a photograph of a famous battle

Visual Support	Contextual Support

184 Reading & Writing Companion

Close Read

✏️ WRITE

INFORMATIVE Write a short paragraph in which you explain the role of the courts in the Hansberrys' fight for justice and the impact of its outcome. Use details from the text and your background knowledge about the American court system. Be sure to include appropriate topic vocabulary in your writing. Pay attention to and edit for pronouns and antecedents.

Use the checklist below to guide you as you write.

☐ What was the outcome of the Hansberrys' first court case?

☐ What did the Hansberrys decide to do after their first case?

☐ What was the outcome of the Supreme Court case?

☐ How did the new outcome ensure everyone has the same opportunity?

Use the sentence frames to organize and write your informative paragraph.

The Hansberrys fought against _____.

The outcome of their first case was that _____.

Then they took their case to the _____.

The second court ruled for _____.

This case helped to end _____.

Home Is Where the Heart Is

DRAMA

Introduction

Tiny homes are small houses, sometimes on wheels, that are built inexpensively and often as charity for the homeless or less fortunate. In this drama, two teenagers explain how their volunteer project means so much more than just an activity to put on a college application. Tiny homes can carry a lot of heart.

VOCABULARY

community
a group of people living in the same place

environment
the natural world

volunteer
a person who works for a cause without getting paid

application
a written formal request or action, usually to join a work or school community

READ

Home Is Where the Heart Is

1 [SCENE: A CAMERAPERSON from Channel 5 News sets up equipment on the lot of a tiny home **community**. It's a breezy, crisp Saturday morning. MR. RAY, the news correspondent, prepares to interview two high school students, OLIVIA and JACKSON.]

2 MR. RAY: (*speaking to the CAMERAPERSON*) Are we ready? Make sure to get the community in the background. Oh, and zoom in on that house they are working on (*points to a tiny, wooden home on wheels*). It is what the story is all about! (*turning to OLIVIA and JACKSON*) How are you kids feeling? Don't be nervous. You'll be great. I'm just going to ask you a few questions about your project.

3 (*OLIVIA and JACKSON shrug and smile slightly, appearing nervous.*)

4 CAMERAPERSON: Three, two, one . . . Action!

5 MR. RAY: (*MR. RAY looks directly into the camera and smiles, gripping his microphone.*) Good morning! This is Daniel Ray from Channel 5 News, live from the new Westmont "tiny home" community. I'm speaking with two extraordinary teenagers who decided to spend their day helping others instead of sleeping in! (*chuckles*) Olivia Wilson and Jackson Lee are two of

Home Is Where the Heart Is

NOTES

Westmont High School's **volunteers** who are building "tiny homes" for the homeless population. Tell me, Olivia, what exactly is a "tiny home"?

6   OLIVIA: It's a small house that we build out of wood. It is also on wheels, so the homeowner can move it wherever he or she wants. Right now, we are setting up these tiny homes here in our community lot.

7   MR. RAY: That's fantastic! It's like a little neighborhood. What else can you tell me about the "tiny home movement"?

8   OLIVIA: Some people might not know this, but Westmont isn't the only community that is doing a project like this. Across America, the tiny home movement is going strong! These homes are super practical and affordable. You can rent one for as little as $200 a month.

9   JACKSON: Also, Olivia and I have been studying the **environment** in our science class, and we learned that tiny homes are actually better for the environment! Tiny homes reduce carbon footprints. That means that these smaller homes use less electricity. We are building these homes for the homeless, but living "smaller" is actually better for everyone! We're trying to get the word out that tiny homes could be the future!

10   MR. RAY: I am very impressed, kids. Jackson, why did you decide to build houses on the weekend? I'm sure there are plenty of other things you could be doing with your time.

11   JACKSON: I guess . . . but this project is actually really enjoyable. Plus, it's rewarding. We get to build homes for people who otherwise might not be able to have them. It's a pretty cool thing to do. And I don't really mind waking up early on the weekends! (*laughs*)

12   MR. RAY: (*laughs along with JACKSON*) That's great. Now, Jackson and Olivia, you are both juniors in high school, correct?

13   (*Both Jackson and Olivia nod.*)

14   MR. RAY: You're at the age when looking at colleges becomes very important. Have any colleges paid attention to your volunteer work and leadership? If I were an admissions counselor, I would definitely want you to attend my college! I bet the likelihood of getting accepted to your first choice school is very high.

15   JACKSON: Well . . . (*trails off, trying to find the right words to say*) I haven't really thought about it. I guess this project is something I can add to my college **applications**.

16 MR. RAY: Absolutely! I'm sure any university would be happy to have you! What about you, Olivia? Are you hopeful that your work will increase your chances of being accepted to your dream school? Is attending a great school your motivation for doing this volunteer work?

17 (*MR. RAY holds the microphone out to OLIVIA, anticipating her response. However, OLIVIA is silent, as if deep in thought.*)

18 MR. RAY: (*laughs nervously, waiting for OLIVIA to respond.*)

19 (*OLIVIA remains silent, but furrows her eyebrows. She appears to be in another world, thinking deeply.*)

20 MR. RAY: Um . . . Let's check in with Jackson about –

21 (*Suddenly, OLIVIA snaps out of her thoughts and takes the microphone from MR. RAY.*)

22 OLIVIA: Excuse me, Mr. Ray and Jackson. But I do have something to say. I hope people don't think Jackson and I, along with the other volunteers, are making these tiny homes to impress universities or get noticed. We are doing this to help others. We are volunteering because it's the right thing to do. We're not asking for attention or fame. We want to make a difference. Plus, speaking from personal experience . . . (*OLIVIA stops talking, looking down at the ground. She seems nervous.*)

23 MR. RAY: Olivia? Do you want to finish what you were about to say?

24 OLIVIA: (*clears her throat*) Yes. This is very personal, but when I was growing up, my family was homeless for a little while. We didn't have any place to go, so we had to live in hotel rooms. Sometimes, we even slept in our car. In school, people teased me for wearing the same shirt or pants two days in a row. I couldn't have any friends over after school. No one knew my secret. (*pauses, looks down*) We didn't have anyone building tiny homes back then. Being able to live in a house like the ones we are building now would have changed my life. I guess that's why I do this. I do this for all of the families who have fallen on hard times. I do it for anyone who needs a second chance. I guess what I'm trying to say is that building these tiny homes isn't about impressing colleges. It's about heart.

25 (*MR. RAY, JACKSON, and the CAMERAPERSON remain silent. Everyone looks at OLIVIA in awe. OLIVIA hands the microphone back to MR. RAY.*)

26 MR. RAY: (*stumbles to find the right words*) That is an amazing story, Olivia. I think I can speak for everyone here in saying that you are quite a remarkable young woman! On behalf of the Westmont community, and Channel 5 News, we thank you, Jackson, and the rest of the volunteers here today. We are grateful for your selflessness and dedication. You're quite an inspiration.

27 (*OLIVIA smiles. JACKSON gives her a high five. The teenagers walk off camera, pick up some tools, and get back to work. MR. RAY looks at them admiringly.*)

28 MR. RAY: This has been Daniel Ray, live from the Westmont tiny home community. Back to you in the studio!

29 *(End of scene)*

Home Is Where the Heart Is

First Read

Read "Home Is Where the Heart Is." After you read, complete the Think Questions below.

☁ THINK QUESTIONS

1. Who are Jackson and Olivia?

   Jackson and Olivia are _____

   _____.

2. Why does Mr. Ray interview Jackson and Olivia?

   Mr. Ray interviews Jackson and Olivia because _____

   _____.

3. Why is building tiny homes for the homeless important to Olivia? Include evidence from the text to support your response.

   Building tiny homes is important to Olivia because _____

   _____.

4. Use context to confirm the meaning of the word *application* as it is used in "Home Is Where the Heart Is." Write your definition of *application* here.

   Application means _____.

   A context clue is _____.

5. What is another way to say tiny homes are better for the *environment*?

   Tiny homes are _____.

Home Is Where the Heart Is

Skill: Analyzing Expressions

★ DEFINE

When you read, you may find English expressions that you do not know. An **expression** is a group of words that communicates an idea. Three types of expressions are idioms, sayings, and figurative language. They can be difficult to understand because the meanings of the words are different from their **literal**, or usual, meanings.

An **idiom** is an expression that is commonly known among a group of people. For example, "It's raining cats and dogs" means it is raining heavily. **Sayings** are short expressions that contain advice or wisdom. For instance, "Don't count your chickens before they hatch" means do not plan on something good happening before it happens. **Figurative** language is when you describe something by comparing it with something else, either directly (using the words *like* or *as*) or indirectly. For example, "I'm as hungry as a horse" means "I'm very hungry." None of the expressions are about actual animals.

••• CHECKLIST FOR ANALYZING EXPRESSIONS

To determine the meaning of an expression, remember the following:

✓ If you find a confusing group of words, it may be an expression. The meaning of words in expressions may not be their literal meaning.

- Ask yourself: Is this confusing because the words are new? Or because the words do not make sense together?

✓ Determining the overall meaning may require that you use one or more of the following:

- context clues
- a dictionary or other resource
- teacher or peer support

✓ Highlight important information before and after the expression to look for clues.

192 Reading & Writing Companion

Read the sentences below. Then, complete the chart by identifying the expression used in each sentence and writing what you think the expression means.

YOUR TURN

	Expression Options
A	"snaps out of her thoughts"
B	"have fallen on hard times"
C	"get the word out"

Sentence	Expression	Meaning
We're trying to get the word out that tiny homes could be the future!		
I do this for all of the families who have fallen on hard times.		
Suddenly, OLIVIA snaps out of her thoughts and takes the microphone from MR. RAY.		

Skill:
Visual and Contextual Support

★ DEFINE

Visual support is an image or an object that helps you understand a text. **Contextual support** is a **feature** that helps you understand a text. By using visual and contextual supports, you can develop your vocabulary so you can better understand a variety of texts.

First, preview the text to identify any visual supports. These might include illustrations, graphics, charts, or other objects in a text. Then, identify any contextual supports. Examples of contextual supports are titles, headers, captions, and boldface terms. Write down your **observations**.

Then, write down what those visual and contextual supports tell you about the meaning of the text. Note any new vocabulary that you see in those supports. Ask your peers and your teacher to **confirm** your understanding of the text.

••• CHECKLIST FOR VISUAL AND CONTEXTUAL SUPPORT

To use visual and contextual support to understand texts, do the following:

- ✓ Preview the text. Read the title, headers, and other features. Look at any images and graphics.
- ✓ Write down the visual and contextual supports in the text.
- ✓ Write down what those supports tell you about the text.
- ✓ Note any new vocabulary that you see in those supports.
- ✓ Create an illustration for the reading and write a descriptive caption.
- ✓ Confirm your observations with your peers and teacher.

YOUR TURN

Read lines 14–19 from "Home Is Where the Heart Is." Then, using the Checklist on the previous page, answer the multiple-choice questions below.

---

from **"Home Is Where the Heart Is"**

MR. RAY: You're at the age when looking at colleges becomes very important. Have any colleges paid attention to your volunteer work and leadership? If I were an admissions counselor, I would definitely want you to attend my college! I bet the likelihood of getting accepted to your first choice school is very high.

JACKSON: Well . . . (*trails off, trying to find the right words to say*) I haven't really thought about it. I guess this project is something I can add to my college **applications**.

MR. RAY: Absolutely! I'm sure any university would be happy to have you! What about you, Olivia? Are you hopeful that your work will increase your chances of being accepted to your dream school? Is attending a great school your motivation for doing this volunteer work?

(MR. RAY *holds the microphone out to* OLIVIA, *anticipating her response. However,* OLIVIA *is silent, as if deep in thought.*)

MR. RAY: (*laughs nervously, waiting for* OLIVIA *to respond.*)

(OLIVIA *remains silent, but furrows her eyebrows. She appears to be in another world, thinking deeply.*)

---

1. This passage provides contextual support by —

   - A. using a chart.
   - B. having Mr. Ray ask questions.
   - C. setting a new vocabulary word in boldface type.
   - D. using a timeline.

2. Based on the stage directions in the passage, the reader can infer that —

   - A. Jackson will likely get into his first choice college.
   - B. Jackson and Olivia think carefully about what they want to say.
   - C. Olivia is silent because she does not know which question to answer first.
   - D. Mr. Ray thinks college is very important.

3. All of the following words provide context clues about the meaning of the boldface word *applications* except —

   - A. motivation.
   - B. college.
   - C. admissions counselor.
   - D. accepted.

Home Is Where the Heart Is

Close Read

✏ WRITE

NARRATIVE: Think about the television interview in "Home Is Where the Heart Is." Write a paragraph in which Jackson and Olivia discuss how they hope the interview will help the tiny homes project in their neighborhood. Use specific examples and details from the play and add some of your own. Be sure to include appropriate topic vocabulary in your writing. Pay attention to and edit for correct spelling when adding suffixes to words ending in silent -e and -y.

Use the checklist below to guide you as you write.

☐ What does Olivia hope the result of the interview will be?

☐ What does Jackson hope the result of the interview will be?

☐ How do Olivia and Jackson feel about the interview?

Use the sentence frames to organize and write your narrative.

After the interview, Jackson tells Olivia that he hopes the interview will show people how _____

tiny homes are. Olivia says that she hopes people will _____

that tiny homes can _____ the lives of homeless people.

Jackson says that the interview will show that anyone can _____

to build tiny homes. The two students are _____ about the interview.

PHOTO/IMAGE CREDITS:

cover, ©iStock.com/MBPROJEKT_Maciej_Bledowski
cover, ©iStock.com/eyewave, ©iStock.com/subjug, ©iStock.com/lvantsov, iStock.com/borchee, ©iStock.com/seb_ra
p. iii, iStock.com/DNY59
p. iv, ©iStock.com/Blackbeck
p. iv, Kate Chopin - Public Domain
p. v, ©iStock.com/Blackbeck
p. v, iStock.com/LdF
p. vi, ©iStock.com/Blackbeck
p. vi, istock.com/fcafotodigital
p. vi, Stock.com/stanley45/
p. vi, iStock.com/Dean Mitchell
p. vi, iStock.com/Wavebreakmedia
p. vi, iStock.com/Rich Legg
p. vii, iStock.com/hanibaram, iStock.com/seb_ra, iStock.com/Martin Barraud
p. vii, iStock.com/oonal
p. ix, ©iStock.com/MBPROJEKT_Maciej_Bledowski
p. x, Paul Laurence Dunbar - Anthony Barboza/Contributor/Archive Photos/Getty Images
p. x, Alice Moore Dunbar-Nelson- Interim Archives/Contributor/Archive Photos/Getty Images
p. x, Charlotte Perkins Gilman - Fotosearch/Stringer/Archive Photos/Getty Images
p. x, Lorraine Hansberry - BTJP1G, Everett Collection Inc/Alamy Stock Photo
p. x, Langston Hughes - Underwood Archives/Contributor/Archive Photos/Getty Images
p. x, Zora Neale Hurston - Archive Photos/Fotosearch/Stringer/Getty Images
p. xl, Yiyun Li - Ulf Andersen/Contributor/Getty Images Entertainment
p. xl, Richard Linklater - Vittorio Zunino Celotto/Staff
p. xl, Edgar Allen Poe - Universal History Archive/Contributor/Universal Images Group/Getty Images
p. xl, Chief John Ross - MPI/Stringer/Archive Photos/Getty
p. xl, August Wilson - Boston Globe/Contributor/Boston Globe/Getty Images
p. 0, ©iStock.com/Boogich
p. 2, Anthony Barboza/Archive Photos/Getty Images
p. 4, Library of Congress/Corbis Historical/Getty Images
p. 7, ©iStock.com/Boogich
p. 8, iStock.com/Gregory_DUBUS
p. 9, Hulton Archive/Stringer/Archive Photos/Getty images
p. 11, ©istock.com/margotpics
p. 16, ©istock.com/margotpics
p. 17, ©iStock.com/ThomasVogel
p. 18, ©iStock.com/ThomasVogel
p. 19, ©iStock.com/fotogaby
p. 20, ©iStock.com/fotogaby
p. 21, ©iStock.com/Brostock
p. 22, ©iStock.com/Brostock
p. 23, ©istock.com/margotpics
p. 24, ©iStock.com/ZargonDesign
p. 29, ©iStock.com/ZargonDesign
p. 30, ©iStock/Spanishalex
p. 31, ©iStock/Spanishalex
p. 32, ©iStockphoto.com
p. 33, ©iStockphoto.com
p. 35, ©iStock.com/ZargonDesign
p. 36, ©iStock.com/DanBrandenburg
p. 37, Public Domain
p. 38, Public Domain
p. 39, Public Domain
p. 40, ©iStock.com/poco_bw
p. 44, ©iStock.com/poco_bw
p. 45, ©iStock/Spanishalex
p. 46, ©iStock/Spanishalex
p. 47, ©iStock/Dominique_Lavoie
p. 48, ©iStock/Dominique_Lavoie
p. 49, ©iStock.com/poco_bw
p. 50, ©iStock.com/
p. 51, Public Domain
p. 53, ©iStock.com/
p. 54, ©iStock.com/
p. 55, ©iStock.com/
p. 57, iStock.com/Orla
p. 58, iStock.com/Orla
p. 59, iStock.com/peepo
p. 60, iStock.com/peepo
p. 61, ©iStock.com/
p. 62, iStock.com/imamember
p. 63, StudySync Image
p. 69, ©iStock.com/DNY59
p. 70, ©iStock/ivan-96
p. 86, ©iStock.com/
p. 94, ©iStock.com/LoraLiu
p. 95, Fotosearch/Archive Photos/Getty Images
p. 113, ©iStock.com/LoraLiu
p. 114, ©iStock.com/Orla
p. 115, ©iStock.com/Orla
p. 116, iStock.com/Martin Barraud
p. 117, iStock.com/Martin Barraud
p. 118, iStock.com/antpkr
p. 123, ©iStock.com/Jcomp
p. 128, ©iStock.com/Jcomp
p. 129, ©iStock.com/Hohenhaus
p. 130, ©iStock.com/Hohenhaus
p. 131, ©iStock.com/Jcomp
p. 132, iStock.com/hanibaram, iStock.com/seb_ra, iStock.com/Martin Barraud
p. 133, iStock.com/Martin Barraud
p. 137, Michael Ochs Archives/Michael Ochs Archives/Getty Images
p. 138, StudySync Graphic
p. 142, ©iStock.com/koya79
p. 145, ©iStock.com/Mutlu Kurtbas
p. 148, ©iStock/DNY59
p. 151, ©iStock.com/Martin Barraud
p. 158, iStock.com/
p. 160, ©iStock.com/horiyan
p. 162, iStock.com/tofumax
p. 164, iStock.com/me4o
p. 166, ©iStock.com/Martin Barraud
p. 168, ©iStock.com/Customdesigner
p. 170, iStock.com/
p. 172, iStock.com/
p. 174, ©iStock.com/Martin Barraud
p. 176, ©iStock.com/DNY59
p. 177, ©iStock.com/dlewis33
p. 177, ©iStock.com/
p. 177, ©iStock.com/baona
p. 177, ©iStock.com/
p. 179, StudySync Image
p. 180, iStock.com/DNY59
p. 181, ©iStock.com/BlackJack3D
p. 183, ©iStock.com/AlexandrBognat
p. 185, ©iStock.com/DNY59
p. 186, ©iStock.com/jax10289
p. 187, ©iStock.com/halbergman
p. 187, ©iStock.com/Wavebreakmedia
p. 187, ©iStock.com/RoBeDeRo
p. 187, ©iStock.com/kavram
p. 191, ©iStock.com/jax10289
p. 192, ©iStock.com/Ales_Utovko
p. 194, ©iStock.com/AlexandrBognat
p. 196, ©iStock.com/jax10289

Please note that excerpts and passages in the StudySync® library and this workbook are intended as touchstones to generate interest in an author's work. The excerpts and passages do not substitute for the reading of entire texts, and StudySync® strongly recommends that students seek out and purchase the whole literary or informational work in order to experience it as the author intended. Links to online resellers are available in our digital library. In addition, complete works may be ordered through an authorized reseller by filling out and returning to StudySync® the order form enclosed in this workbook.

Text Fulfillment Through StudySync

If you are interested in specific titles, please fill out the form below and we will check availability through our partners.

ORDER DETAILS

Date:

TITLE	AUTHOR	Paperback/ Hardcover	Specific Edition *If Applicable*	Quantity

SHIPPING INFORMATION

Contact:
Title:
School/District:
Address Line 1:
Address Line 2:
Zip or Postal Code:
Phone:
Mobile:
Email:

BILLING INFORMATION ☐ SAME AS SHIPPING

Contact:
Title:
School/District:
Address Line 1:
Address Line 2:
Zip or Postal Code:
Phone:
Mobile:
Email:

PAYMENT INFORMATION

☐ CREDIT CARD

Name on Card:

Card Number:	Expiration Date:	Security Code:

☐ PO

Purchase Order Number:

StudySync Text Fulfillment, BookheadEd Learning, LLC
610 Daniel Young Drive | Sonoma, CA 95476